ROUTLEDGE LIBRARY EDITIONS:
INTERNATIONAL BUSINESS

BRITISH MANUFACTURING INVESTMENT OVERSEAS

BRITISH MANUFACTURING INVESTMENT OVERSEAS

DAVID SHEPHERD, AUBREY SILBERSTON AND
ROGER STRANGE

Volume 35

Routledge
Taylor & Francis Group

LONDON AND NEW YORK

First published in 1985

This edition first published in 2013
by Routledge
2 Park Square, Milton Park, Abingdon, Oxon, OX14 4RN

Simultaneously published in the USA and Canada
by Routledge
711 Third Avenue, New York, NY 10017

Routledge is an imprint of the Taylor & Francis Group, an informa business

British Library Cataloguing in Publication Data
A catalogue record for this book is available from the British Library

ISBN: 978-0-415-63009-2 (Set)
eISBN: 978-0-203-07716-0 (Set)
ISBN: 978-0-415-65776-1 (Volume 35)
eISBN: 978-0-203-07654-5 (Volume 35)

Publisher's Note
The publisher has gone to great lengths to ensure the quality of this reprint but
points out that some imperfections in the original copies may be apparent.

Disclaimer
The publisher has made every effort to trace copyright holders and would
welcome correspondence from those they have been unable to trace.

Printed and bound by CPI Group (UK) Ltd, Croydon, CR0 4YY

British
Manufacturing Investment
Overseas

David Shepherd, Aubrey Silberston
and Roger Strange

METHUEN

London and New York

First published in 1985 by
Methuen & Co. Ltd
11 New Fetter Lane, London EC4P 4EE

Published in the USA by
Methuen & Co.
in association with Methuen, Inc.
733 Third Avenue, New York, NY 10017

Typeset by Activity Ltd, Salisbury, Wilts
Printed in Great Britain at the University Press, Cambridge

British Library Cataloguing in Publication Data
Silberston, Aubrey
British manufacturing investment overseas.
1. Investments, British
I. Title   II. Shepherd, David, *1952–*
III. Strange, Roger
332.6'7341   HG4538

ISBN 0-416-39490-6

Library of Congress Cataloging in Publication Data
Silberston, Aubrey.
British manufacturing investment overseas.
Bibliography: p.
Includes index.
1. Investments, British.
I. Shepherd, David.   II. Strange, Roger.
III. Title.
HG4538.S467   1985   332.6'7341   85-124

ISBN 0-416-39490-6

Contents

List of tables   vii
List of figures   ix
Preface   xi

1   Preliminary remarks   1

2   Overseas investment: statistical background   5

I   Introduction   5
II   Preliminary data considerations   8
III   Geographical analysis   9
IV   Sectoral analysis   12
V   International comparisons   19
VI   Inward investment in the United Kingdom   21
VII   The financing of direct investment   25
VIII   Concluding remarks   27

3   Overseas investment: analytical background   31

I   Trade and investment   31
II   The firm and overseas production   35
III   Some macroeconomic considerations   45
IV   The development of international firms   50

4   Historical developments in overseas investment   53

I   Trade, protection and overseas investment   53
II   Post-war developments   59
III   Changes in domestic economic structure   62
IV   Summary   68

5   The sample of firms   69

I   The composition of the sample   69
II   The coverage of the sample   73
III   The company interviews and the questionnaire   76

Contents

6   Why do firms manufacture overseas?
     Some preliminary evidence   **79**

          I Servicing foreign markets   80
          II Questionnaire responses   82
          III Concluding comments   97

7   Why do firms manufacture overseas?
     Evidence from the case studies   **101**

               I The industries   101
          II Food, drink and tobacco   102
               III Electrical engineering   107
     IV Chemicals (including pharmaceuticals)   114
          V Mechanical and instrument engineering
     (including motor vehicle components)   121
     VI Mechanical engineering (construction)   131
     VII Textiles, leather, clothing and footwear   133
          VIII Paper, printing and publishing   136
                    IX Other manufacturing
          (including metal manufacture)   138

8   Concluding comments on overseas manufacturing
               investment   **147**

               I Introduction   147
     II The nature of overseas manufacturing   148
     III The causes of overseas manufacturing   151
          IV Investment overseas as a substitute for
                    investment in the UK   154
          V Consequences of overseas manufacturing
                    investment   156

          References   163
               Index   169

Tables

2.1 Stock of direct investment abroad of developed market economies by major country of origin, 1967–76   6

2.2 United Kingdom external assets – investment by the private sector   7

2.3 UK outward direct investment by main world area (excluding oil companies, banks and insurance companies)   10

2.4 Book value of UK outward direct investment in manufacturing, distribution and the 'resource-based' industries by main areas at end 1965–81 (excluding oil companies, banks and insurance companies)   15

2.5 Sectoral distribution of UK outward direct investment in manufacturing industry   18

2.6 Structure of foreign direct investment of selected countries by broad industrial sector at end of 1978   20

2.7 Structure of foreign direct investment in manufacturing of selected countries by industrial sector at end of 1971   22

2.8 Inward direct investment flows of developed market economies (percentage distribution among thirteen countries)   23

2.9 UK manufacturing industry – sectoral distribution of outward and inward direct investment at end of 1981   24

4.1 UK outward direct investment and exports by world area   61

4.2 Sectoral distribution of UK overseas assets in manufacturing   63

4.3 Net output by UK manufacturing industry (% of total)   64

4.4 Trade balance by industry   65

4.5 Trade balance and value-added in electrical engineering   67

5.1 Sectoral distribution of UK outward direct investment by manufacturing industry at the end of 1978 (excluding oil companies, banks and insurance companies)   70

5.2 Size distribution of company sample in terms of net assets employed, turnover and trading profit in 1980   74

5.3 Geographical analysis of turnover, trading profit and employment of company sample, 1980 (excluding anonymous companies)   75

6.1 What do you think are the main advantages that your

company (or product) possesses which enable it to compete with foreign or indigenous firms overseas?   83

6.2   What factors attracted your company to the overseas market?   84

6.3   Before production facilities were established in Country X, how was the market serviced?   85

6.4   What important factors influenced the decision to service the overseas market by overseas production?   86

6.5   What products does your company produce overseas?   88

6.6   If overseas production had not been established in Country X would it have been possible for you to establish or continue export sales to Country X or to license production?   91

6.7   Are your overseas affiliates organized as essentially independent businesses or as integrated parts of an international Group operation?   93

6.8   Are your overseas subsidiaries and branches allowed a large degree of autonomy? To what extent are their pricing, marketing, etc. decisions subject to approval by central management?   95

6.9   How does your company organize its R & D activities? Is product or process research and development centrally located or spread across affiliates?   96

6.10 What control does the parent company exercise over its overseas affiliates with regard to further investment by the affiliates?   97

8.1   Identified effect on the balance of payments of direct investment overseas (excluding oil companies)   158

Figures

2.1 Geographical analysis of UK net outward direct investment
1959–81 (three-year moving averages)   12

2.2 Sectoral analysis of UK net outward direct investment
1959–81 (three-year moving averages)   14

2.3 Components of net outward direct investment by UK
companies 1959–81 (three-year moving averages)   26

2.4 Gross flows of UK outward direct investment 1958–81   28

Preface

This book presents the results of a study of British manufacturing investment overseas. The work was undertaken while the authors were all members of the Department of Social and Economic Studies at Imperial College, and was financed by a grant from the Anglo-German Foundation for the Study of Industrial Society.

The project was under the general direction of Aubrey Silberston and David Shepherd. The detailed design of the study was largely in the hands of David Shepherd, who also made the principal contribution to the final text. All three authors were, however, actively involved in the execution of the project and the final result represents a collaborative effort.

Our thanks are due to the Anglo-German Foundation who generously financed the study. It had been intended that a parallel study should be carried out for overseas investment by German firms, but unfortunately our collaborators in Germany were unable to complete their study. Secondly, we wish to thank the company executives who gave us their time in discussing the experiences of their respective firms. Finally, we wish to record our gratitude to Brian Price and Angela Hallett who helped us tremendously in the preparation of the manuscript.

David Shepherd
Aubrey Silberston
Roger Strange

CHAPTER ONE

Preliminary remarks

The study which we present here is an attempt to elaborate the causes of British direct investment overseas in manufacturing industry. In doing this we follow the usual notion that direct investments are those which involve the investor in a significant degree of managerial control of the overseas enterprise, as opposed to portfolio investments in which the investor acts in the manner of a *rentier*. Although a significant part of total overseas investment is composed of portfolio investment, we have concentrated exclusively on direct investment since its explanation is less straightforward than portfolio investment and its impact has perhaps more interesting ramifications for the domestic economy. There exists a well developed body of financial analysis – portfolio theory – which would seem to give, in so far as one can ever claim such a thing, an adequate explanation of portfolio investment. In the case of direct investment, however, we are faced with a less settled analysis and one which draws upon perhaps debatable aspects of economic theory, particularly in relation to the analysis of the firm.

Direct investment can in its turn be sub-divided into the rough categories of investment in manufacturing, in distribution, in primary activities such as mining, and in services. While we give some consideration to each of these components, by far our greatest attention is given to overseas investment in manufacturing. Our reason for this, again, is that it seems desirable to concentrate on that category which is inherently the most interesting, particularly in its implications for the domestic economy, and the least straightforward in its explanation. As it happens, this consideration is strengthened by the fact that overseas investment in manufacturing represents by far the largest proportion of total direct investment and the one which has shown the greatest growth over the period we have studied – the years since the Second World War.

Our study contains a number of comments on the theory of overseas investment, but in general the material is of an empirical nature and is to a large degree derived from case studies of a selected sample of British firms. Before we outline the general direction of the work, however, we should indicate why a study of this kind seems appropriate.

1

British Manufacturing Investment Overseas

Over recent years there has been a considerable number of empirical studies of overseas investment. Summaries of the coverage and details of the most important studies have been provided by Hood and Young (1979) and Caves (1982), and we need mention here only those problems which seem of particular importance in relation to our own work. In the first place, the majority of empirical studies have been of a statistical nature and have attempted to identify certain common features shared by firms with foreign subsidiaries (which we shall refer to as international firms). At the risk of generalizing, the most important findings of these statistical studies are that, within an industry, international firms tend to be larger and more diversified than purely domestic firms, and tend in particular to have some combination of a greater research and development intensity, a greater advertising intensity, and a greater capital intensity. The difficulty is, however, that while this line of investigation is extremely useful in highlighting these common shared characteristics, the aggregative nature of the statistical evidence limits its ability to differentiate further between alternative hypotheses and to distinguish potentially important detail. For example, quite apart from the possibility that the factors mentioned might be a reflection of some other underlying characteristics of international firms, it seems that some factors (for instance research and development expenditure) are also significant in explaining the propensity of firms to export (see for instance Hood and Young 1979, pp. 156–9). While this may suggest, as for instance Dunning (1980) has argued, that the explanation of trade and direct investment flows are part of a more general theory of international production, it also indicates the need for a more detailed study of investing firms to bring out a greater degree of micro-economic detail. Similarly, to take another example, many large firms produce a range of goods within an industry and are both significant exporters and overseas manufacturers. In order to identify any important differences between production locations of products it is necessary to examine the firms in some depth.

There have of course been several previous studies of international firms (see the summary in Dunning 1973), but these have usually concentrated on only a limited number of the many aspects of overseas investment – for example, they have often neglected the alternatives to overseas investment. From our perspective, however, perhaps the most important deficiency of these studies is that they have been concerned almost exclusively with the behaviour of US firms. Since one cannot necessarily suppose that the experience of US firms is readily transferable to the UK, a study of British firms is clearly necessary. The only satisfactory way to obtain the level of detail required to understand a firm's overseas investment strategy is to use a case study approach. Unfortunately, in adopting this approach there is a trade-off, in that the detail of the investigation necessarily limits the number of firms which can be studied. Because of this, it is possible that one may gain a distorted view of the subject. We discuss this problem in a later chapter, but at this point we note that our own feeling is that we have gained a reasonably representative view of the range of motives for overseas manufacturing investment. In the last resort, however, such an objection to the case study method is impossible to counter completely, and for the unconvinced the case study material must be taken as interesting examples of the overseas investment behaviour of some important British companies.

In the following two chapters we present a general, background picture of the statistics relating to British direct investment overseas and the theories which have been put forward to explain this investment. The statistical chapter is intended to survey the most important trends in overseas investment. It highlights the sectoral, industrial and geographical changes which have taken place over the post-war years. Since the subject of the book is outward investment flows from the UK, we have given only the briefest attention in the statistics to inward investment and to overseas investment by firms based in other countries. We believe that this is preferable to a rather half-hearted coverage of subjects which require a full treatment if they are to be discussed properly. The analytical chapter, on the other hand, is not intended to be a survey. Good surveys have been provided elsewhere and would merely be duplication here. What we have attempted is to draw together those aspects of previous theoretical work which seem to us particularly important, and to present them in a manner which gives a realistic framework for examining the historical development of British foreign investment. No doubt this will not satisfy those who believe in the importance of particular explanations to which we may have decided to give little weight.

Chapter 4 is a preliminary to the main case study chapters and consists of a brief examination of the historical development of British overseas direct investment, from its origins in the late nineteenth century through to the post-war period. This chapter emphasizes the close relationship between British trade and British overseas investment, and the way in which current investment patterns depend upon previous historical developments.

The chapters which follow contain the main case study material and consist of evidence on the nature and causes of overseas investment, obtained from interviews with the senior management of our sample companies and from a general questionnaire which they were asked to complete. In general the evidence is concerned with the period from the mid-1960s onwards and concentrates on investment in the areas of greatest importance during this period – particularly Western Europe, the United States and, to a lesser degree, the 'Old Commonwealth'. However, given that it is unrealistic to separate these investments from those in other areas and those which were undertaken in earlier periods, the latter are not excluded from examination. The final chapter of the book then draws together some of our main conclusions and ends by briefly considering the question of the consequences for the British economy of overseas direct investment.

As a final comment, we should perhaps note the differences between our work and the major case study work on British firms carried out by Professor Reddaway (1968). Aside from the fact that our sample of firms is smaller than that examined by Reddaway, the major differences concern the scope and method of analysis. Much of the Reddaway report was concerned with an analysis of financial statistics, gathered from firms, in an attempt to estimate the quantitative impact of overseas investment on the balance of payments: the causes and alternatives to overseas investment were for the most part a subsidiary matter. We, on the other hand, have reversed this order of priority and have given only subsidiary attention to the consequences for the British economy of overseas investment. Because of this we have adopted a different approach from that of Reddaway and have concentrated on evidence of a qualitative nature, concerned with the strategy of firms. Our hope however is that there exists a degree of complementarity between the two studies.

CHAPTER TWO

Overseas investment: statistical background

I Introduction

The main purpose of this chapter is to provide a summary of the basic statistics relating to outward direct investment by UK enterprises. Direct investment in this context refers to

> investment that is made to add to, to deduct from, or to acquire, a lasting interest in an enterprise other than that of the investor, the investor's purpose being to have an effective voice in the management of the enterprise. Other investments in which the investor does not have an effective voice in the management of the enterprise are mainly portfolio investments. (HMSO 1982, p. 28)

The United Kingdom has historically had much larger holdings of overseas direct investments than most other industrialized countries. As Table 2.1 shows, the bulk of international direct investment is attributable to a very small number of countries. Between them, the United States, the United Kingdom, Germany, Japan, Switzerland and France accounted for 83 per cent of the total stock in 1976. Notwithstanding their pre-eminent position, it is clear that the relative shares taken by the United States and the United Kingdom have been declining as a consequence of the more rapid growth of direct investment from other countries, particularly Germany and Japan. The share of the United States fell steadily from 53.8 per cent at the end of 1967 to 47.6 per cent at the end of 1976. The comparable figures for the United Kingdom show an even more marked reduction; from 16.6 per cent of the total stock at the end of 1967, to 11.2 per cent only at the end of 1976. Meanwhile, the German share more than doubled from 2.8 to 6.9 per cent while that of Japan increased almost five-fold from 1.4 to 6.7 per cent.

The Central Statistical Office publishes, in the 'Pink Book', annual estimates of the external assets and liabilities of the United Kingdom. Table 2.2 summarizes the assets held by the private sector at the end of

5

Table 2.1 Stock of direct investment abroad of developed market economies by major country of origin, 1967–76

Country of origin	Percentage distribution, end of				
	1967	1971	1973	1975	1976
United States	53.8	52.3	51.0	47.8	47.6
United Kingdom	16.6	15.0	13.5	11.9	11.2
Germany	2.8	4.6	6.0	6.2	6.9
Japan[1]	1.4	2.8	5.2	6.1	6.7
Switzerland	4.8	6.0	5.6	6.5	6.5
France	5.7	4.6	4.4	4.3	4.1
Canada	3.5	4.1	3.9	4.1	3.9
Netherlands	2.1	2.5	2.8	3.2	3.4
Sweden	1.6	1.5	1.5	1.7	1.7
Belgium–Luxembourg	1.9	1.5	1.4	1.2	1.2
Italy	2.0	1.9	1.6	1.3	1.0
Total above	96.2	96.8	96.9	94.3	94.2
All others (estimate)	3.8	3.2	3.1	5.7	5.8
Grand total	100.0	100.0	100.0	100.0	100.0

Source: OECD (1981) *International Investment and Multinational Enterprises: Recent International Direct Investment Trends*, Paris, OECD, p. 39.

Note: 1   Fiscal year beginning 1 April of the year indicated.

certain selected years. Banking and other claims (which amounted to £25,141 million at the end of 1981) are not included.

As can be seen, direct investment has accounted for a large proportion of UK private investment overseas over the last twenty years, typically about two-thirds of the total. One should note that the size of the portfolio investment stock has trebled since the abolition of exchange control in 1979. Exchange control was not designed to restrict profitable direct investment, and this has shown little sign of any marked increase in real terms since 1979. The data on the book values of direct investments in industries other than oil, banking and insurance are obtained from the periodic (1962, 1965, 1968, 1971, 1974, 1978 and 1981) Census inquiries conducted by the Department of Trade. The figures show that direct

Table 2.2   United Kingdom external assets – investment by the private sector (balance, end year, £ million)

Year	Direct		Portfolio	Miscellaneous[1]	Total
	excluding oil, banks and insurance companies	total			
1962	3,405.0	4,870	3,200	–	8,070
1965	4,210.0	n.a.[2]	n.a.	–	n.a.
1968	5,585.3	7,800	6,150	–	13,950
1971	6,666.9	9,127	6,100	–	15,227
1974	10,435.8	14,465	5,700	–	20,165
1978	19,107.7	26,856	10,100	710	37,666
1979	n.a.	30,765	12,000	900	43,665
1980	n.a.	34,125	18,000	950	53,075
1981	28,545.1	43,496	24,400	1,440	69,336
1982	n.a.	50,959	37,900	1,720	90,579

Sources: *Census of Overseas Assets 1981*, Business Monitor MA4, 1981 Supplement, London, HMSO, 1984, pp. 12–13; *United Kingdom Balance of Payments* (various editions), London, HMSO.

Notes: 1   Included with direct investment by oil companies prior to 1975.
2   n.a. = not available.

investment grew at an average rate of 8 per cent per annum at current prices between 1962 and 1971, but that the rate doubled to 16 per cent between 1971 and 1978. The major factor behind this change was the higher rate of inflation in the 1970s. This not only increased the cost of new investment but also caused some existing assets to be revalued upwards. The fall in the value of sterling over the period also contributed to the increase in the sterling value of overseas assets. The rate of growth has slackened a little since 1978.

At the end of 1981 – the latest year for which the Department of Trade has published detailed figures (HMSO 1984, p. 38) – there were 1509 UK enterprises (excluding oil companies, banks and insurance companies) engaged in overseas direct investment. Between them they had interests in 9092 overseas affiliates of which 3612 were located in Western Europe (HMSO 1984, pp. 16–17, 38), 1239 in North America, 1332 in the 'Other Developed' countries (essentially Australia, New Zealand, South Africa and Japan) and the remaining 2909 in the 'Rest of the World'. The total book value of this direct investment was slightly over

£28.5 billion. Of these 1509 UK enterprises engaged in direct investment, the majority (1177) had overseas interests whose book value did not exceed £5 million. Taken together, these affiliates accounted for less than 2.5 per cent of the total book value. In contrast, a mere thirty-four companies, each with over £200 million invested overseas, were responsible for nearly 56 per cent of the total book value of net assets held. Unfortunately, a detailed regional breakdown by size of UK overseas investment is not available.

Following this brief overview of the significance of UK direct investment overseas, we will concentrate in the rest of this chapter on its evolution over the last twenty years or so. In particular, we will try to examine changes in its geographical and sectoral composition, to compare the experience of the United Kingdom with that of other industrialized countries, to contrast the pattern of outward investment with that of inward investment, and to indicate how overseas investment is financed.

II Preliminary data considerations

There are two sets of geographically and sectorally disaggregated data which describe the evolution of direct investment overseas by the United Kingdom.

The first set records direct investment *flows* and is obtained from annual inquiries carried out by the Department of Trade, the Bank of England and the British Insurance Association. These inquiries are conducted primarily for balance of payments purposes and deal therefore with financial flows and changes in indebtedness. Direct investment is defined as the amount of finance provided by parent companies to their overseas affiliates (the figures exclude the transactions of government departments and oil companies but include a number of public corporations) and can take the form of either retained profits, acquisition of share and loan capital, or short-term credit loans. It should be noted that this definition of direct investment is not the same as either the growth in a company's net assets or capital expenditure on fixed assets. Direct investment refers only to the money invested in a related concern by the parent company. That concern then decides how to use the money, for example to repay borrowing or to acquire fixed assets. Moreover, a related concern can also raise funds locally without recourse to its parent or associate.

The investment flows entered under 'UK private direct investment overseas' in the capital account of the balance of payments refer to transactions taking place within particular periods. Such transactions affect the stock of external assets and liabilities, and an analysis of such stocks can yield an alternative perspective on the direct investment position of the United Kingdom. Information on the book value of net assets is provided by (usually) triennial inquiries carried out by the Department of Trade and covers all industries except oil, banking and insurance. Again, it is important to realize that the stock of overseas direct investment is not the same as the value of fixed assets. The book value of direct investment covers only the money invested by the parent company. This can be greater than the value of fixed assets held by a subsidiary, branch or associate if part of the investment is used to finance working capital, or less if some of the fixed assets are financed by local borrowing. Moreover, changes in the stock of external assets do not necessarily correspond exactly to the transactions recorded in the intervening period. Apart from the cumulative value of net investment, there will be adjustments for exchange rate movements, revaluations of assets and, more recently, changes in the method of accounting for deferred tax which has had the effect of increasing the value of net assets due to the net investor.

Stocks of net assets are measured at book values. These usually refer to the price paid for the assets when originally purchased, often many years in the past, but occasionally show the worth of the assets when last revalued. The book value will thus typically be lower than replacement cost or market value, especially in times of inflation, although book values can exceed the realizable market value at times of economic depression.

Both flow and stock data can, in principle, be used to provide sectoral and geographical analyses of the overseas investment position of the United Kingdom. The data on direct investment flows are, however, subject to considerable annual fluctuations due to short-term changes in indebtedness/extraordinary acquisitions, etc. which tend to obscure the underlying trends in net asset growth. For these reasons, it is preferable to use the statistics on the book value of net assets. These figures provide a reasonable indication of external capital formation, although the qualifications mentioned above should be borne in mind. Data on investment flows are provided as supporting evidence where they are thought to be helpful.

III   Geographical analysis

The first comprehensive geographical analysis of the stock of UK direct investment abroad was provided by the Department of Trade for the end of 1962. For periods before this inquiry, the available information is rather sketchy but Houston and Dunning provide some (apparently comparable) data for the end of 1929. These figures (Table 2.3) show

9

Table 2.3 UK outward direct investment by main world area (excluding oil companies, banks and insurance companies)

	Percentage of total book value of assets at end year								
	1929	1962	1965	1968	1971	1974	1978	1981
Western Europe	7.4	13.4	15.4	17.6	21.9	27.5	31.2	23.2
North America	7.3	23.1	21.8	23.0	22.0	21.8	25.2	34.6
Other developed	10.9	27.1	29.9	30.8	29.8	30.1	23.2	20.4
Total (Developed)	25.6	63.5	67.1	71.5	73.7	79.3	79.6	78.2
Rest of World	74.4	36.5	32.9	28.5	26.3	20.7	20.4	21.8
Total (World)	100.0	100.0	100.0	100.0	100.0	100.0	100.0	100.0
Total (£ million)	1551.0	3405.0	4210.0	5583.3	6666.9	10435.8	19107.7	28545.1

Sources: Houston, T. and Dunning, J. H. (1976) *UK Industry Abroad*, London, Financial Times Ltd., p. 113; *Census of Overseas Assets 1981*, Business Monitor MA4, 1981 Supplement, London, HMSO, 1984, pp. 12–13.

that only a small proportion of UK direct investment overseas in 1930 was located in the developed countries: Europe accounted for 7.4 per cent, North America for 7.3 per cent and the 'Other Developed' countries, for 10.9 per cent. About three-quarters was concentrated in the 'Rest of the World' (particularly South and Central America, and the Far East).

Between 1930 and 1962 there was a considerable redistribution of capital, mainly as a result of the loss or sale of companies in non-Commonwealth countries and the concentration, after the Second World War, on new projects within the Commonwealth. Houston and Dunning (1976) estimate that about 80 per cent of recorded UK direct investment overseas between 1946 and 1960 was in Commonwealth countries, and much of this was in Australasia, Canada and South Africa. By the end of 1962 the share of UK net assets located in the developed countries had risen to over 60 per cent, of which 27 per cent was held in the 'Other Developed' countries. The share taken by North America was about a quarter of the total, with Canada accounting for half as much investment again as the United States, and a mere 13 per cent was held in the countries of Western Europe. The eight largest recipient countries at the end of 1962, ranked by book value of net assets, were Australia, Canada, USA, South Africa, India, Malaysia, New Zealand and Nigeria – all in the Commonwealth but the USA.

Heavy investment by UK enterprises in Western Europe and the United States ensued in subsequent years and, by the end of 1978, the share of total net assets located in Western Europe had risen to over 30 per cent. The flow of investment to Western Europe was particularly strong in the years at the end of the 1960s and the beginning of the 1970s. After 1972, investment in Western Europe declined fairly steadily as a percentage of the annual total whereas investment in North America (particularly the United States) increased substantially. By the end of 1978, the United States had taken over from Australia as the principal recipient of UK direct investment overseas and, by the end of 1981, over a third of UK assets were located in North America (of which 28 per cent was located in the United States). Although the flow of investment to Western Europe declined in relative terms during the latter half of the 1970s, at the end of 1981 over 23 per cent of the stock of assets overseas were located on the Continent (see Figure 2.1).

Over the last twenty years, therefore, the increases in the relative importance of Western Europe and, more recently, the United States have been achieved at the expense of a fall (from 37 per cent at the end of 1962 to 22 per cent at the end of 1981) in the share of UK direct investment located in the 'Rest of the World'. The 'Other Developed' countries have also declined in importance quite markedly since the end of the 1960s. India, Malaysia, New Zealand and Nigeria have been

11

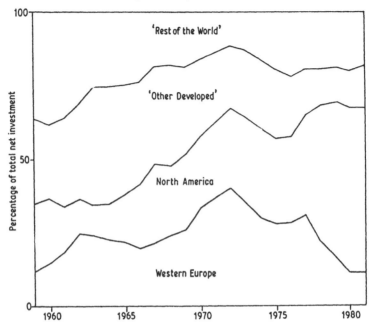

Figure 2.1 Geographical[1] analysis of UK net outward direct investment[2], 1959–81 (three-year moving averages)

Sources: 1958: *Board of Trade Journal* (19 April 1963) p. 880; 1959: *Board of Trade Journal* (7 August 1964) p. 289; 1960–1: *Board of Trade Journal* (2 April 1965) p. 733; 1962–5: *Overseas Transactions 1968*, Business Monitor M4, Table 16; 1966–71: *Overseas Transactions 1976*, Business Monitor MA4, pp. 10–11; 1972–82: *Overseas Transactions 1982*, Business Monitor MA4, pp. 12–13.

Notes: 1 See text for further details of geographical classification. Japan included in 'Rest of World' before 1966.
2 Excluding oil companies.

replaced in the list of the eight largest recipient countries by Germany, Netherlands, France and Hong Kong.

IV Sectoral analysis

The geographical redistribution of UK assets overseas has been accompanied by a sectoral redistribution. In the late nineteenth and early twentieth centuries, most of the UK capital invested in overseas business had gone into new companies which had been formed to exploit sources of raw materials or to supply transport and other infrastructure investment (Edelstein 1982). Investment in overseas manufacturing facilities increased during the inter-war period, although the emphasis was still on the primary and service industries. Sir Robert Kindersley (1939) reported that 7 per cent of UK capital invested in British companies operating abroad in 1938 was in manufacturing or distribution facilities. The primary or 'resource-based' industries (oil, mines, nitrates, agriculture) accounted for 31 per cent and the service industries (railways, utilities, communications, financial, etc.) for the remaining 62 per cent.

Considerable disinvestment had taken place in Latin America (in railways, utilities, land, etc.) in the early 1930s and there were also severe losses during and after the Second World War. Houston and Dunning estimate that more than 40 per cent of total overseas business assets were lost through destruction, expropriation, nationalization or sale during the period 1939 to 1956. Nevertheless, in the post-war period, there was a marked rise in the flow of foreign direct investment, particularly for the establishment of manufacturing and distribution facilities. By the end of 1962, 51 per cent of the book value of UK companies' direct investment abroad was in manufacturing industry and a further 13 per cent in distribution outlets. The share taken by the primary industries (agriculture and mining, but excluding oil) had fallen to 20 per cent (see Appendix for a detailed industrial classification).

Figure 2.2 illustrates the relative development of these three aggregate industrial groupings (Manufacturing, Distribution, and Agriculture and Mining) by reference to annual investment flows since the beginning of the 1960s. As can be seen, around 50 per cent of the annual flow of UK direct investment overseas (excluding oil) over the last twenty years has been in manufacturing industry. Until the mid-1970s, the proportion exhibited a gentle upward trend but this was interrupted somewhat in the latter half of the decade by heavy investment in industries classified as 'Other non-manufacturing' (i.e. construction, transport, property and financial). Meanwhile, the share of investment taken by the primary industries has declined dramatically, particularly since the end of the 1960s, while that directed to distribution facilities has remained fairly constant. Table 2.4 provides a geographical analysis of these overall trends by reference to the stocks of assets held in each specified area. The stock figures exclude not only the assets of oil companies, but also those of the banks and insurance companies. Direct investment by the latter is included in the annual flow data from which Figure 2.2 was constructed. This explains why, for example, manufacturing only accounts for about 50 per cent of the annual flow, but a larger proportion of the total stock of UK direct investment overseas. Figures are expressed as percentages of the total book value of net assets held in each specified geographical area. Hence, at the end of 1981, 60.6 per cent of direct investment in the developed countries was in manufacturing, 12.5 per cent in distribution and 7.2 per cent in agriculture and mining – the remaining 19.7 per cent was in construction, transport, etc.

13

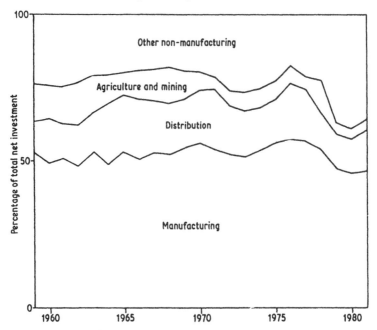

Figure 2.2 Sectoral[1] analysis of UK net outward direct investment[2], 1959–81 (three-year moving averages)

Sources: 1958: *Board of Trade Journal* (19 April 1963) p. 882; 1959: *Board of Trade Journal* (7 August 1964) p. 291; 1960: *Board of Trade Journal* (19 July 1968) p. xii; 1961–5: *Board of Trade Journal* (9 May 1969) p. 1311; 1966–71: *Overseas Transactions 1972*, Business Monitor M4, Part I, p. 21; 1972–4: *Overseas Transactions 1975*, Business Monitor M4, pp. 36–7; 1975–7: *Overseas Transactions 1979*, Business Monitor MA4, pp. 30–1; 1978–82: *Overseas Transactions 1982*, Business Monitor MA4, pp. 34–5.

Notes: 1 By industrial activity of overseas affiliate. See text and Appendix for further details of industry classification.
2 Excluding oil companies.

As we have already suggested, the relative importance of manufacturing as the objective of UK direct investment overseas increased steadily during the 1960s and early 1970s. In 1965, manufacturing affiliates accounted for only 50 per cent of the total book value of UK direct investment. By 1978 this proportion had grown to 63.2 per cent, largely at the expense of the 'resource-based' industries whose share of total investment had declined markedly, particularly during the 1970s. After 1978 manufacturing declined in relative importance as proportionately more investment was made in property and financial activities. Nevertheless, manufacturing has remained the most important compo-

Table 2.4   Book value of UK outward direct investment in manufacturing, distribution and the 'resource-based'[1] industries by main areas at end 1965–81 (excluding oil companies, banks and insurance companies)

Area and industry of overseas affiliate	Percentage of total book value of net assets at end year in each specified geographical area					
	1965	*1968*	*1971*	*1974*	*1978*	*1981*
Western Europe						
Manufacturing	49.6	57.1	66.7	61.9	57.3	57.2
Distribution	29.5	29.3	18.2	24.3	23.1	16.5
Agriculture and mining	–[2]	–	–	1.6	–	–
North America						
Manufacturing	59.7	60.3	68.2	59.6	74.3	64.3
Distribution	17.1	16.3	8.8	15.3	13.1	12.3
Agriculture and mining	10.0	–	14.5	–	–	–
Other developed countries						
Manufacturing	59.7	61.4	62.9	62.3	65.6	58.2
Distribution	8.5	10.8	9.9	10.3	12.0	8.2
Agriculture and mining	–	–	–	–	13.0	–
Total: developed countries						
Manufacturing	57.4	60.0	65.6	61.4	65.2	60.6
Distribution	16.1	17.1	12.0	16.5	15.4	12.5
Agriculture and mining	8.1	10.4	11.1	8.8	5.3	7.2
Rest of world						
Manufacturing	34.8	34.4	40.6	47.5	55.1	42.5
Distribution	15.6	16.2	16.3	17.1	21.0	16.8
Agriculture and mining	29.1	30.0	25.7	19.5	9.4	13.9
World						
Manufacturing	50.0	52.7	59.0	58.6	63.2	56.6
Distribution	15.9	17.1	13.1	16.7	16.5	13.4
Agriculture and mining	15.1	16.0	15.0	11.1	6.1	8.6

Sources: *Board of Trade Journal* (26 January 1968) pp. ix–x; *Board of Trade Journal* (23 September 1970) p. 647; *Overseas Transactions*, Business Monitor M4, Part II, 1972, London, HMSO, 1974, pp. 10–13; *Census of Overseas Assets 1974*, Business Monitor M4, 1974 Supplement, London, HMSO, 1977, pp. 8–11; *Census of Overseas Assets 1978*, Business Monitor MA4, 1978, London, HMSO, 1981, pp. 10–15; *Census of Overseas Assets 1981*, Business Monitor MA4, 1981, London, HMSO, 1984, pp. 18–23.

Notes: 1   Agriculture, forestry and fishing; mining and quarrying.
2   Symbol – signifies that the figure is suppressed to avoid disclosure of information relating to individual enterprises.

nent of direct investment and at the end of 1981 still accounted for over 56 per cent of the total stock of assets. Meanwhile, the proportion of investment allocated to distribution appears to have remained fairly constant over the whole period at around 13–17 per cent of the total.

These overall trends conceal some interesting variations which only become apparent when the disaggregated figures for the major geographical areas are considered. In Western Europe, the share of total assets taken by manufacturing rose significantly during the latter half of the 1960s and reached a peak of 66.7 per cent at the end of 1971. This movement was accompanied by a fall in the importance of distribution facilities to 18.2 per cent. Similar trends are apparent for North America but, whereas the relative importance of manufacturing investment in Europe appears to have declined a little during the 1970s, in North America it increased in importance (to 74.3 per cent of the total at the end of 1978) before subsequently falling back.

The proportion of investment devoted to distribution facilities is highest in Western Europe, although the importance of the sector has declined over time relative to manufacturing. In 1965 the respective shares of UK direct investment in Western Europe taken by manufacturing and distribution were 49.6 and 29.5 per cent. The gap between the two widened considerably during the later years of the 1960s so that by the end of 1971 the corresponding figures were 66.7 and 18.2 per cent. By the end of 1981, however, the relative proportions were slightly closer – 57.2 and 16.5 per cent. North America and the 'Other Developed' countries, on the other hand, show a much larger proportion of investment in agriculture and mining. UK investment in 'resource-based' industries in Western Europe accounted for only 1.6 per cent of the total at the end of 1974.

As regards the 'Rest of the World', the importance of the resource-based sector has declined markedly from 29.1 per cent at the end of 1965 to only 13.9 per cent at the end of 1981. This decline has been accompanied by increased investment in manufacturing, particularly up to the end of 1978. It is interesting to note that there has been a significant change in the pattern of investment in the developing countries. In 1965 the manufacturing and 'resource-based' sectors were of comparable size. By 1981 the former accounted for over three times the book value of assets held in the latter. There is a similar shift of emphasis in the developed countries but it is not nearly as strong. Nevertheless, manufacturing still accounts for a much smaller percentage of total investment in the developing countries (42.5 per cent at the end of 1981) than it does in the developed countries (60.6 per cent at the end of 1981).

A more detailed breakdown of the sectoral changes that have taken place in UK outward direct investment in manufacturing industry is not possible since such analyses have only been published for the last

16

four Censuses. However, a rough assessment can be made by comparing statistics for the end of 1955 from the sample used in the Reddaway report with Census data from the end of 1981. The two sets of data are not exactly comparable: in particular, the Census data are disaggregated according to the 1968 revision of the Standard Industrial Classification, so that Reddaway's classification cannot, by definition, be the same. Moreover, Reddaway's data were based on a sample of companies and no estimates are available for the firms not included: there is thus no basis to judge whether the sample constitutes a truly representative cross-section of manufacturing industry. Reddaway (1968, pp. 139–40) did, however, estimate that his sample had a coverage of 71 per cent of British manufacturing industry at the end of 1962. Finally, the Census figures are based on 'net assets of overseas subsidiaries, branches and associates attributable to UK companies' which differs from Reddaway's use of the 'book value of the UK stake' in that the latter does not include non-current liabilities or the assets of associated companies.

Notwithstanding these and other finer points of definition (in particular, see Reddaway's own discussion of these matters, pp. 139–40), it is still evident (see Table 2.5) that there have been significant changes in the sectoral composition of UK direct investment abroad over the twenty-six year period considered. At the end of 1955 the predominant sector for UK manufacturing investment overseas was Food, drink and tobacco which accounted for almost half of the total book value of the 'UK stake'. Next in importance came Chemicals and allied industries (11.9 per cent); Textiles, leather, clothing and footwear (8.1 per cent); Motor vehicles (7.9 per cent) and Metal manufacture (7.3 per cent). The sector which was most poorly represented was Mechanical and instrument engineering with less than 2 per cent. By the end of 1981, the picture had changed quite considerably. Food, drink and tobacco was no longer the most important sector and it now accounted for only just over a quarter of the total book value of net assets in manufacturing industry. Three other sectors showed a reduction in their share of total investment: Metal manufacture, Motor vehicles, and Textiles. In contrast, three sectors showed a marked increase in their relative importance: Chemicals and allied industries (which with 28 per cent of total manufacturing assets was the most important sector at the end of 1981), Mechanical and instrument engineering, and Electrical engineering.

Dunning (1981) attempts to classify the above industrial groupings according to whether they are more or less technology intensive on the basis of their research and development (R & D) expenditure as a percentage of net output. More technology intensive industries are defined as those which spent 2 per cent or more of their net output on research and development and less technology intensive industries as those which spent less than 2 per cent. Thus Chemicals and allied

Table 2.5 Sectoral distribution of UK outward direct investment in manufacturing industry[1] (percentage of total)

Industry of overseas affiliate	Reddaway sample[2] book value of 'UK stake' at end 1955	Census of overseas assets book value of net assets at end 1981
Food, drink and tobacco	47.3	27.1
Chemicals and allied industries	11.9	28.0
Metal manufacture	7.3	2.0
Mechanical and instrument engineering	1.9	6.3
Electrical engineering	5.4	10.0
Motor vehicles	7.9	3.4
Textiles, leather, clothing and footwear	8.1	4.3
Paper, printing and publishing	5.4	5.5
Other manufacturing[3]	4.7	13.4
Total	100.0	100.0
Total (£ million)	750.2	16,166.9

Sources: Reddaway, W. B. in collaboration with Potter, S. J. and Taylor, C. T. (1968) *Effects of UK Direct Investment Overseas* (Final Report) University of Cambridge, Department of Economics, Occasional Paper 15, CUP, p. 362; *Census of Overseas Assets 1981*, Business Monitor MA4, 1981 Supplement, London, HMSO, 1984, pp. 18–23.

Notes: 1 See text for discussion of comparability of sources.
2 Industry classification of Reddaway sample is only approximate.
3 Including 'rubber'.

industries, Mechanical and instrument engineering, Electrical engineering, Motor vehicles and Rubber are labelled as 'more technology intensive' industries; Food, drink and tobacco, Metal manufacture, Textiles, and Paper as 'less technology intensive' industries. On this division, the above figures appear to suggest that, since the end of 1955, there has been a tendency for UK direct investment overseas to be increasingly in the 'more technology intensive' sectors of manufacturing industry.

One should however be careful when drawing such conclusions from the data. The subtleties of the industrial classification will be discussed in more detail in chapter 5 when we describe the construction of our company sample, but at this point we should note that the broad aggregation of industries by SIC Order conceals a wide range of diversity within each category. For example, the category 'Mechanical and instrument engineering' includes some industries (mechanical handling equipment; industrial plant and steelwork) where R & D expenditure is relatively low as well as others (instrument engineering) where such expenditures is high. There is no way of knowing, from the aggregate statistics, which is the most prominent in terms of overseas investment. Moreover, one should consider the extent to which the sectoral changes in UK direct investment overseas were accompanied by concomitant developments in the domestic economy. On the one hand, the tendency towards investment in the 'more technology intensive' industries may have reflected changes in the UK economy as a whole. On the other, it may have been an independent trend. These questions will be considered further in chapter 4 below.

V   International comparisons

We have seen that the United Kingdom has historically had much larger holdings of overseas direct investment than other industrialized countries, apart from the USA. It is also true to say that there are important differences in terms of both geographical location and sectoral distribution.

The OECD (1981, p. 47) provide statistical information on the stock of overseas investment at the end of 1976 attributable to manufacturing companies from the four most important investing nations – the United States, the United Kingdom, Germany and Japan. These figures show that a high proportion of the overseas manufacturing assets of the United States, the United Kingdom and Germany (over 80 per cent for the US and the UK; over 70 per cent for Germany) are concentrated in the developed countries. In contrast, the majority (73 per cent) of Japanese overseas investment is in the developing nations. Using similar data for 1971, Morgan (1979, p. 79) points out that German investment is concentrated (52 per cent) in Europe, particularly in the EEC, whereas a large proportion (33 per cent) of UK assets were in the developed countries of the Commonwealth. The situation with regard to the geographical distribution of UK assets is changing, as we saw earlier (pp. 9–12). In the case of American overseas investment, about a third is located in Canada.

The corresponding sectoral analysis is shown in Table 2.6. Care should be taken when interpreting the figures because the bases for their

Table 2.6 Structure of foreign direct investment of selected countries by broad industrial sector at end of 1978 (percentage of total)

	United Kingdom	United States	Germany	Japan
Manufacturing	46.7	44.5	42.0	32.4
Distribution	13.2	9.8	18.3	14.2
Mining and petroleum	26.3	26.8	4.4	28.4
Other	13.8	18.9	35.3	25.0
Total	100.0	100.0	100.0	100.0

Source: OECD (1981) *International Investment and Multinational Enterprises: Recent International Direct Investment Trends,* Paris, OECD, pp. 47, 76.

compilation are not strictly comparable (see Morgan, 1979, pp. 78–80). Nevertheless, the following general remarks may be made. It appears that the proportion of total overseas investment devoted to manufacturing industry (42–6 per cent) is about the same for the United Kingdom, the United States and Germany. German firms, however, invest much less in the mining and petroleum industries than do their counterparts in the other three selected countries, but more in distribution facilities. In contrast, less than a third of Japanese investment abroad is in manufacturing and a similar proportion is in mining and petroleum. The broad sectoral patterns of overseas investment by UK and US enterprises are very similar – manufacturing accounting for about 45 per cent of the total, distribution 10–13 per cent, and mining and petroleum 26 per cent. These aggregate figures, however, conceal significant sectoral differences within manufacturing industry. Both American and German investment is concentrated in the 'more technology intensive' industries (see Table 2.7). Morgan, again using data for the end of 1971, estimates that the share of total German manufacturing investment in the Chemicals, Mechanical engineering, Electrical engineering and Motor vehicles, etc. sectors was 68.1 per cent. The corresponding figure for US investment was only slightly less at 64.6 per cent. In contrast, British and Japanese investments were still predominately in the 'less technology intensive' industries: their shares in the 'more technology intensive' industries were lower, at 39.2 and 38.7 per cent respectively. We should also note in passing that a large proportion of the difference between the United Kingdom, and the USA and Germany is accounted for by the relative absence of overseas investment in motor vehicle manufacture by UK firms. The figures for chemicals, electrical and mechanical engineering are closer across the three countries.

VI Inward investment in the United Kingdom

The evidence presented in the previous section suggests that the pattern of UK direct investment overseas has historically been qualitatively different from that of the other major industrialized countries. This observation is of interest when one comes to examine inward investment by such countries into the United Kingdom. Not only does Britain have the second largest stock of overseas assets, it has also been historically a major recipient of international direct investment flows. Over the period 1961 to 1967, the United Kingdom was the fifth most important host country (see Table 2.8) for direct investment flows into OECD countries, taking 9.7 per cent of the total behind Germany (21.3 per cent), Canada (16.2 per cent), Australia (15.6 per cent) and Italy (11.5 per cent).

Table 2.7 Structure of foreign direct investment in ma   acturing of selected countries by industrial sector at end of 1971 (percentage of total)

	United Kingdom	United States	Germany	Japan
Chemicals	17.4	16.5	30.8	6.8
Mechanical engineering	6.7	15.7	9.6	9.5
Electrical engineering	12.7	10.0	15.5	10.2
Motor vehicles and other transport equipment	2.4	22.4	12.2	12.2
	39.2	64.6	68.1	38.7
Food, drink and tobacco	28.1	–	3.8	7.1
Metals	3.6	7.4	8.1	19.2
Textiles, etc.	7.6	–	2.6	26.4
Other	21.5	–	17.4	8.6
Total	100.0	100.0	100.0	100.0

Source: Morgan, A. D. (1979) 'Foreign manufacturing by UK firms', in Blackaby, F. (ed.) *De-industrialisation*, London, Heinemann, pp. 78–94.

Table 2.8 Inward direct investment flows of developed market economies (percentage distribution among thirteen countries)

Host country	1961–7	1968–73	1974–9
United States	2.6	11.4	26.7
France	8.2	8.2	15.2
Germany	21.3	16.4	14.7
Australia	15.6	12.9	9.5[1]
Belgium	4.5[2]	6.1	9.4
United Kingdom	9.7	7.4	6.1
Netherlands	4.7	8.5	6.0[3]
Italy	11.5	8.3	5.0
Norway	0.8	1.4	4.1
Spain	2.7	3.7	3.7
Canada	16.2	12.1	3.2
Japan	2.0	1.7	1.2
Sweden	2.4	1.7	0.5[4]

Source: OECD (1981) *International Investment and Multinational Enterprises: Recent International Direct Investment Trends*, Paris, OECD, p. 41.

Notes:
1 1974–6
2 1965–7
3 1974–8
4 1974–7

However, by the mid-1970s, this picture had changed dramatically. Within Europe, there had been significant increases in the shares of Belgium and France and concomitant decreases in those of Germany, Italy and the United Kingdom. Elsewhere Australia and Canada also suffered decreased shares but the most striking change was the increased role of the United States as a recipient of international direct investment. During the period 1974 to 1979, the United States accounted for 26.7 per cent of the total, followed by France (15.2 per cent), Germany (14.7 per cent), Australia (9.5 per cent), Belgium (9.4 per cent) and the United Kingdom (6.1 per cent).

Inward investment into the United Kingdom has been overwhelmingly attributable to the United States. At the end of 1981, US companies were responsible for over 56 per cent of total book value of £16,962.0 million (cf. the figure of £28,545.1 million for the book value of UK investment overseas) of foreign assets in the United Kingdom (HMSO 1984, p. 41). The next most important country was Switzerland with 7 per cent. Table

Table 2.9 UK manufacturing industry – sectoral distribution of outward and inward direct investment at end of 1981

	Percentage of total book value of net assets in manufacturing industry	
	UK assets overseas	Foreign assets in UK
More technology intensive sectors		
Chemicals and allied industries	28.04	19.70
Electrical engineering	10.03	14.39
Mechanical and instrument engineering	6.27	17.79
Rubber	3.42	2.88
Motor vehicles	3.29	10.61
Total	51.04	65.38
Less technology intensive sectors[1]		
Food, drink and tobacco	27.12	16.49
Other manufacturing[2]	10.09	6.34
Paper, printing and publishing	5.47	5.44
Textiles, leather, clothing and footwear	4.28	0.98
Metal manufacture	1.98	5.37
Total	48.96	34.62
Total manufacturing	100.00	100.00

Source: *Census of Overseas Assets*, Business Monitor MA4, 1981 Supplement, London, HMSO, 1984, pp. 18–23, 46–7.

Notes: 1 Dunning defines 'more technology intensive' sectors as those which 'spent at least 2 per cent of their net output on research and development in 1974; LTI (less technology intensive) industries spent a lower percentage.' Dunning, J. H. (1981) *International Production and the Multinational Enterprise*, London, George Allen & Unwin, p. 174.
2 Including 'shipbuilding, marine engineering and vehicles other than motor vehicles'.

2.9 shows the distribution of this investment by industrial sector. The table indicates that at the end of 1981 only 35 per cent of foreign assets in the United Kingdom were in 'less technology intensive' sectors whereas the comparable figure for UK assets abroad was 49 per cent.

VII   The financing of direct investment

Having considered the geographical and sectoral distribution of direct investment overseas by UK enterprises, we examine in this final section how these investments have been financed. While the method of finance has important implications for the balance of payments, we postpone discussion of this matter until our final chapter on the consequences of overseas investment. At this stage we present information on the relative importance of different categories of finance to give an additional perspective on overseas investment flows.

Annual data on 'UK private direct investment overseas' are recorded in the capital account of the balance of payments. The data refer to changes in indebtedness between UK parent companies and their overseas affiliates and, as such, do not give a complete picture of changes in the total net assets of the affiliates. For example, an overseas affiliate may itself borrow money in order to finance net asset growth, but this would not be included in the annual direct investment flow statistics.

If we leave the above qualification aside, and concentrate on the annual investment flows, we can see that direct investment may essentially take one of three forms:

i)   profits retained overseas by subsidiaries and associates;
ii)   the net acquisition of share and loan capital by the UK parent;
iii)   changes in indebtedness on inter-company or branch–head office account.

The relative importance of these components of investment can be seen in Figure 2.3. Unremitted profits have historically dominated overseas investment flows since 1958 (the first year for which direct investment data were separately identified in the balance of payments) but have fallen off considerably in importance since 1976. The peak years were 1967 and 1976 and these coincide with the years when the share of total investment accounted for by the net acquisition of share and loan capital was at its lowest. The third component, changes in branch indebtedness and in inter-company accounts (essentially amounts due to/from the UK parent company from/to its overseas affiliates in respect of trade credit, short-term loans, etc.), can be seen to have steadily declined in relative importance over the period, reflecting the gradual move away from the branch form of organization.

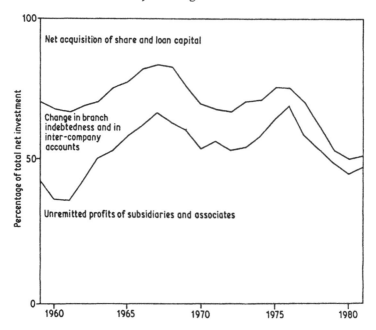

Figure 2.3 Components of net outward direct investment by UK companies[1], 1959–81 (three-year moving averages)

Sources: 1958–9: *United Kingdom Balance of Payments 1968*, p. 24; 1960–6: *Overseas Transactions 1978*, Business Monitor MA4, pp. 6–7; 1967–71: *Overseas Transactions 1981*, Business Monitor MA4, pp. 6–7; 1972–82: *British Business* (18 May 1984) p. 37.

Note: 1   Excluding investment by oil companies, but including investment by a number of public corporations.

Exchange control regulations were in force over most of the period which we are considering (they were eventually abolished in 1979). At this stage, we can note that these regulations may well have influenced the pattern of finance of overseas direct investment by restricting the outflow of funds from the United Kingdom and by encouraging the repatriation of overseas profits. The purpose and effects of the exchange control regulations are discussed further in chapter 8.

Finally, we should note that while direct investment is recorded net in the balance of payments, this does not mean net of investment in the United Kingdom by overseas parent companies – which is referred to as inward investment. Rather, net investment overseas is the result of transactions by UK enterprises in both outward and inward directions. There are many possible measures of gross investment – a completely gross figure would not be particularly meaningful, but one measure commonly used is

> the sum of all the accounting components in which investment was made during each company's year of account, whether the net outcome for any affiliate is positive or negative, and whether or not one component offsets another in the same affiliate. Loans and credits which are both extended and repaid during the course of the accounting year are not included.

Gross investment, thus defined, can take the form of unremitted profits, the purchase of share and loan capital, or an increase in indebtedness to the United Kingdom on inter-company or branch–head office account. Gross disinvestment, on the other hand, comprises unremitted losses including dividends in excess of profits, sales and redemptions of share and loan capital, and any decrease in indebtedness to the United Kingdom on inter-company or branch–head office account. Figure 2.4 shows how gross investment, gross disinvestment and net investment defined in this way have fluctuated over the period 1958 to 1981, measured as a percentage of Gross National Product. It can be seen that net investment overseas has steadily increased in importance relative to GNP from 0.7 per cent in 1958 to 2.5 per cent in 1981. By contrast, the corresponding time paths of gross investment and gross disinvestment show much more volatility, particularly in the 1970s.

VIII   Concluding remarks

The purpose of this chapter has been to provide a summary of the basic statistics relating to outward direct investment by UK enterprises. We have shown that the United Kingdom has over the years been both a major source of, and also an important host to, international direct investment flows. We have also seen that the traditional pattern of such investment has been changing. Increasingly, UK overseas investment has been directed away from the countries of the Old Commonwealth and towards the more developed markets of Western Europe and North America. In conjunction with this geographical redistribution, a large proportion of new investment has been carried out by enterprises in the 'more technology intensive' sectors of UK manufacturing industry. Why these developments have been taking place, and what effects they have had on the domestic economy, are questions which will be examined in subsequent chapters.

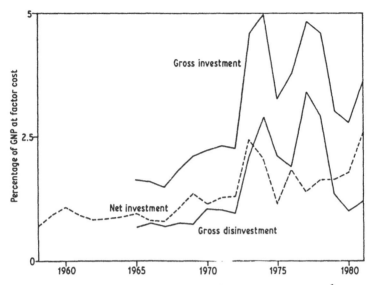

Figure 2.4   Gross flows of UK outward direct investment[1], 1958–81

Sources:
(GNP)   1958–9: *National Income and Expenditure*, 1980 edition, pp. 2–3; 1960–81: *National Income and Expenditure*, 1982 edition, pp. 2–3.
(Investment) 1965: *United Kingdom Balance of Payments 1968*, p. 45; 1966–7: *United Kingdom Balance of Payments 1970*, p. 56; 1968: *United Kingdom Balance of Payments 1970*, p. 53; 1969–71: *United Kingdom Balance of Payments 1973*, p. 50; 1972: *Overseas Transactions 1972*, Business Monitor M4, Para 1, p. 10; 1973: *United Kingdom Balance of Payments 1966–76*, p. 63; 1974: *United Kingdom Balance of Payments 1967–77*, p. 62; 1975–8: *Overseas Transactions 1978*, Business Monitor MA4, pp. 16–17; 1979–81: *Overseas Transactions 1981*, Business Monitor MA4, pp. 12–13.

Notes: 1 Excluding oil companies. For banking and insurance, only net figures were, in general, available. Gross figures are not available before 1965.

Appendix: Industry classification

Returns to the *Census of Overseas Assets* are coded according to the type of business of the companies' affiliates. The industrial analysis of outward investment relates to the activities of the overseas concerns, and that of inward investment to the business of the UK affiliates.

The following twenty industry groups are separately identified:

Manufacturing industries

   i   Food, drink and tobacco
  ii   Chemicals and allied industries

28

  iii Metal manufacture
  iv Mechanical engineering and instrument engineering
   v Electrical engineering
  vi Shipbuilding and vehicles other than motor vehicles
 vii Motor vehicle manufacture
viii Textiles, leather, clothing and footwear
  ix Paper, printing and publishing
   x Rubber
  xi Other manufacturing industries

Non-manufacturing industries

   xii Agriculture, forestry and fishing
  xiii Mining and quarrying
  xiv Construction
   xv Transport and communications, other than shipping
  xvi Shipping
 xvii Distributive trades
xviii Financial services, other than banking and insurance
  xix Property owning and managing
   xx Other activities

A similar classification is used in *Overseas Transactions* for annual investment flows except that banking and insurance are included under 'Other non-manufacturing activities'. See *Overseas Transactions 1980* (Business Monitor MA4, London, HMSO, 1982, p. 5) for a full description of the industrial classification used.

CHAPTER THREE

Overseas investment: analytical background

In this chapter we set out the theoretical background to our study of manufacturing investment overseas. Since there are several good reviews of the overseas investment literature (particularly Hood and Young 1979, and Caves 1982) we have not attempted here an exhaustive coverage of the many contributions to the theory of overseas investment. The chapter is, rather, an attempt to provide an analytical background against which the overseas investment strategies of firms can be considered.

I Trade and investment

The explanations of direct investment overseas which have evolved over the last twenty years have consisted of an application of the theory of the firm to an international context. The traditional theories of international trade, based upon David Ricardo's law of comparative advantage and the Hecksher–Ohlin thesis of factor intensity, could be extended to allow for the pure (portfolio) export of capital, but they proved unsatisfactory in explaining the existence of foreign direct investment. The essential difficulty is that while the Ricardian and Hecksher–Ohlin approaches attribute the existence of trade to some general aggregative characteristic of the trading countries – differences in factor productivities and factor endowments – the source of this comparative advantage is not really explained. Since the comparative advantages are left lying, as it were, with the country, there is no satisfactory way of explaining why the firms of one country should wish, or be able, to set up profitable production in another country, particularly since the alternative of portfolio investment is available. The simple step which allows an explanation of foreign direct investment to be developed comes with the obvious but important recognition that it is the firms in a particular country (as embodiments of labour, capital and entrepreneurship) which display any comparative advantage, and that the microeconomic source of this advantage is to be found not only in general aggregative factors relevant to the country in

31

question, but also in the shape and characteristics of the firms themselves.

The application of the theory of the firm to the problem of foreign direct investment came in two independent but related developments. The first of these (associated in particular with Lindler 1961, and Dreze 1960) stems from the inability of traditional trade theory to account not only for direct investment, but also for the presence of extensive intra-industry international trade. This latter phenomenon is explained by emphasizing microeconomic variations in demand and production in countries of broadly similar industrial development. For instance, to take the example of, say, automobiles, a number of European countries have a substantial motor industry and we can assume that production is, or was, initially directed at supplying cars which embodied the particular performance or stylistic characteristics of their own national markets. On the assumption that there exists a minority taste for such characteristics in other countries (or that this can be generated by advertising) there is a clear possibility that trade in cars will occur between countries. So long as there exists some spare capacity in the respective domestic car industries, helped by economies of scale in production, there is scope for the domestic car industry to supply an overseas 'fringe' market by exporting. Or to change the example, it is not so much that a country has a comparative advantage in the production of television sets, but that some of its firms have acquired an advantage in the production of particular kinds of television sets – for instance, Japanese expertise in the manufacture of small-size televisions.

An alternative explanation for trade concentrates on the role of the firm as an innovator, either in new products or new processes (for instance, Vernon 1966, and Posner 1961). According to this view, a firm which innovates will initially supply its home market, but there will be possibilities for exporting also, at least until firms in foreign countries take up the new process or product. In so far as firms in certain countries are associated with a continual stream of innovations (stimulated in part by the existing social and educational structure) exports of new products will continue to be important to the trade of those countries. While the innovative success of a country may be tied to a particular industry (such that it maintains a dominant position in that area of world production) it may be just as likely that the variety of innovations which occur in an industry or product group are spread across competing countries – with the result that trade in, say, electrical engineering involves two-way trade between countries. Of course, within this general scheme, developments may be more concentrated in certain countries than in others, with the strong position of the United States in many industries being the obvious example.

The importance of this work in trade theory for the analysis of overseas investment is that once it is accepted that comparative advantage is in part a microeconomic phenomenon which rests with the firm, it becomes possible to allow for production strategies other than exporting. In other words, once the firm is admitted explicitly into the argument, it becomes possible that the firm may adopt a strategy for supplying foreign markets in which production need not be tied to its country of origin.

In close parallel with developments in the theory of trade, various authors, concerned with overseas investment and production, have advanced views of the emergence of overseas demand which are similar to those already discussed, but which have been extended to allow for the possibility of foreign production. The notable early contributions in this category include those of Kindleberger (1969), Hymer (1960), Caves (1971, 1974), Vernon (1966, 1979) and Johnson (1970). In essence, their approach is to suggest that in a world of perfect competition it would be impossible to explain how a firm could compete in a foreign country, since it would have no advantage over indigenous firms, and indeed, in practice, would face a number of disadvantages due to unfamiliarity with local laws, markets, customs and so on. Their explanation of why firms can compete in foreign markets is based upon market imperfections, and the associated barriers to entry, which give the firm advantages over indigenous competitors in other countries. The typical market imperfections which give rise to these advantages are those which are often associated with monopolistic or oligopolistic firms – to give a few examples: the acquisition of patents and other restricted information derived particularly from research and development expenditure; special managerial or marketing skills; access to capital markets; and differentiated products.

. Later work, particularly of a statistical nature, has tended to confirm that international firms do indeed seem to derive their comparative advantages from such factors as the possession of intangible knowledge and differentiated products (reflected in above average research and development and advertising intensity), the benefits of size, scale economies, and so on (see Dunning 1980, and Caves 1982, for a summary of the evidence). The problem with this kind of evidence, however, is that while it supports the theoretical work on overseas investment, it is also consistent with explanations of why trade, and in particular intra-industry trade, takes place. It has become apparent therefore that those theories of trade and foreign direct investment which rely upon an analysis of the firm are in reality part of a common explanation of why firms are attracted to, and are able to compete in, foreign markets (for instance Dunning 1980). In order to explain why market servicing takes the form of overseas production rather than exporting it is necessary to supplement the analysis with those locational considerations which influence the firm. These may take the form of cost considerations (such as transport costs, tariff barriers or wage costs) or demand considerations (such as the need for adaptability of product specification or after-sales servicing, or political buying restrictions) which make it necessary or more profitable for the firm to source production abroad (see Horst 1973 for an analysis of cost factors). A frequent suggestion is that for many products the typical sequence of events is one in which the firm initially supplies an overseas market by exporting and at a later stage (perhaps because market size and competition have increased and the product price has fallen, so that cost factors or tariffs become significant) begins to develop an overseas manufacturing facility (see for instance Vernon 1966, 1974, and Buckley and Casson 1981).

Before we leave this discussion and move on to consider another possibility – that of licensing as an alternative to exporting and overseas production – we should make one further brief observation. So far, we have followed the drift of much of the theoretical literature by analysing the behaviour of the firm in a relatively static context in which it is, implicitly, comparing the potential for exporting with the establishment of a new manufacturing facility overseas. While this approach is of great help in isolating the various factors which influence the investment decision, and in highlighting the close relationship between exporting and overseas production, it is necessary to allow for more 'dynamic' considerations in order to develop a realistic picture of the behaviour of overseas investment.

It was the important insight of Penrose (1956) that there may be a difference between analysing the establishment of a new overseas subsidiary and the growth of an already existing subsidiary. Penrose's suggestion – that already established subsidiaries are better analysed in the context of the growth of the firm, rather than the theory of foreign investment – is less pertinent in the light of the emphasis placed upon the firm in subsequent work on foreign investment, but the recognition was nevertheless still important. In any 'real world' analysis of overseas investment we are for the most part dealing with a situation of growth, and one in which a significant part of foreign direct investment consists of an expansion of existing facilities. This implies that we should allow for any important influences derived from the theory of the growth of the firm. Perhaps of most importance, however, is that any attempt to understand the current pattern of overseas investment must make due allowance for the historical context of the firm's evolution. In particular, one must recognize that decisions which the firm takes today may be heavily influenced by the decisions it took in previous periods. Many current investment decisions would be difficult to understand unless due allowance were made for the 'inertia' which is introduced by the presence of existing overseas production facilities.

In part this inertia may stem from the heavy fixed investment (both human and physical) which is implied by existing overseas facilities. To take a simple example: the firm may have established an overseas subsidiary during an earlier period when tariff barriers in a particular country were high and wage costs were relatively low. Although the tariff may have been subsequently removed, and wage costs have risen, so that the firm would be indifferent or dissuaded from setting-up in that country today, the existing investment and experience of production may make it most efficient (or easier) to maintain and expand production in its present location. Additionally, one might expect a degree of inertia in the firm's location strategy to stem from less straightforward considerations. Once a subsidiary of some size has been established overseas, it may acquire to a degree a 'life of its own', to use Penrose's phrase, which introduces a bias towards its retention (or expansion) which is greater than the static analysis might imply. And while sufficiently adverse changes in costs, etc., might eventually lead to a movement in production to another location, the inertia induced by past investment may at the very least cause considerable delay before this adjustment takes place.

II The firm and overseas production

Up to this point, we have taken it for granted that we are concerned with explaining direct manufacturing investment overseas and that the alternative to this form of market servicing is exporting from the firm's domestic base. Non-manufacturing investment overseas seems to be more readily explained. For example, to take the two most important categories of non-manufacturing investment overseas, investments connected with raw material extraction and related primary activities must usually be located at or near the source of the material, while investments in distribution facilities must be in the vicinity of the market. For all forms of direct investment, however, recent work has emphasized that it is necessary also to consider why the domestic firm should establish a foreign activity as opposed to conducting the activity via 'arm's length' market transactions. In the case of manufacturing one must explain why the firm does not license production to already existing foreign indigenous firms; in the case of primary activities, such as mining, why it controls production overseas; and in the case of distribution investments, why it does not sell in overseas markets via agents.

The most popular explanation of why external market transactions may be replaced by administered transactions within the firm is based upon Coase's (1937) analysis of transactions costs. This has been developed most recently by Williamson (1973, 1975) and extended to the question of overseas investment by Buckley and Casson (1976). Such has been the popularity of the argument that it is now regarded by many as the proper explanation of the origin and growth of the firm and, extended to overseas investment, as *the* explanation of international firms (Buckley and Casson 1976, Caves 1982) or as an integral part of a more general explanation (Dunning 1980). Before we comment on this development it is helpful to present the essential features of the approach.

In brief, Coase's argument runs that in the absence of firms all transactions would take place on an arm's length, contractual basis, but this series of individual market exchanges would, in a world of imperfect markets, involve heavy costs (particularly in discovering the relevant prices of exchange). Firms, however, greatly reduce these marketing and transactions costs by, in effect, establishing one contract between the factors of production and the entrepreneur: within the limits of this contract a whole series of market contracts are avoided because the factors agree to be directed by the entrepreneur. Thus, the existence and structure of the firm can be explained by the internalization, within a *hierarchical* structure, of a variety of transactions which would be costly or impossible to organize using traditional *market* structures.

While the internalization argument has been developed most completely by Williamson (1973, 1975), for our purposes the application of the idea to overseas investment by Buckley and Casson (1976) is of more immediate relevance. The important aspect of Buckley and Casson's interpretation is their consideration of why a firm may internalize various transactions associated with proprietary rights, rather than license these rights in an external market.

Given that there exists a demand for the firm's products (whether they be final or intermediate products) it is conceivable that the firm could sell or lease its proprietary rights or advantages. In the case of overseas trading, this would involve the firm entering into contractual commitments with foreign producers which, in effect, would sell them the rights to manufacture, using the firm's designs or processes. The argument, in general, is that these contractual relationships may not be established because the relevant markets are highly imperfect. The most important imperfections are deemed to be the lack of organized futures markets, uncertainties connected with the value of knowledge (particularly concerning the valuation of intermediate products or processes), and difficulties in exercising efficient price discrimination in certain external markets. These factors suggest that there would be great difficulties involved in negotiating a licensing contract because of a lack of clearly definable prices, for both the present and the future, which could be mutually agreed. The factors mentioned – particularly when coupled with bilateral concentrations of market power (which lead to unstable bargaining situations) and national differences in fiscal arrangements (which make transfer pricing profitable) – provide prime motivations for the internalization of contracting within the firm's own hierarchy. Internalization allows the contracting problems to be solved by, in effect, giving both parties to the contract a mutual and co-operative interest in the outcome because they are part of the same hierarchy.

Although we have some criticism to make of this analysis of the overseas investment decision, we should say that the approach of Buckley and Casson, and those who have followed, has been extremely useful in highlighting some previously neglected aspects of the subject. Apart from the fact that it has reinforced the notion that the behaviour of firms is paramount in any analysis of overseas investment, it has also emphasized the importance of considering why licensing takes place and why it is not more prevalent. Stemming from this, the internalization approach has been an important stimulus to a consideration of alternative forms of market servicing in the context of a general theory of overseas production (Dunning 1980). Our criticism, such as it is, concerns the matter of whether the analysis of transactions costs should occupy such a prominent position in the explanation of overseas direct investment.

There are two levels at which one can view the analysis of internalization as applied to the problem of overseas investment. The first concerns the more general question of whether one accepts the Coase–Williamson analysis of transactions costs as the 'true' explanation of the origin and growth of the firm. In many ways this is the most important question, since by adopting a particular 'view of the world' one immediately conditions one's analysis of overseas investment, by emphasizing those aspects which stem from that view. The second level of criticism is a more direct one and concerns the question of whether, on their own terms, the detailed arguments of the transactions cost approach give a plausible explanation of overseas investment. We shall consider both levels of the argument, but the latter is more easily dealt with after we have considered the transactions cost view of the origin of the firm.

The origin of the firm

Coase's analysis of the firm implicitly follows an intellectual method which has a long history. The method utilizes a 'thought experiment' which posits a 'state of nature' in which the institution in question does not exist (in Coase's case individual market exchange in the absence of firms) and then asks what failings of the state of nature caused the institution to arise (for Coase, transactions costs). To digress for a moment, an instructive example of the use of this method appears in the seventeenth century (when the method was particularly popular) in *Leviathan* by Thomas Hobbes. In *Leviathan*, the existence of government is explained as a result of a voluntary contract between citizens and a protective sovereign, in which the former agree to submit to the authority of the sovereign in return for relief from the anarchy and constant war which would prevail in the state of nature when government was absent.

37

For Hobbes, however, there was no real suggestion that a voluntary contract of this kind had ever been established in historical reality. He was, as it were, constructing a myth which could explain how rational man might solve a fundamental problem of human organization.

Now, with regard to Coase's analysis of transactions costs, one could take this also as a myth. Its value would then lie not in a literal explanation of how firms have evolved, but as one form of ideal against which to judge the current shape and characteristics of the firm (in the same way, for example, that perfect competition stands as an ideal in Paretian welfare economics). It would seem, however, that the transactions cost argument has been presented, and has been developed, not as a myth of this kind, but as an actual explanation of the historical evolution of the firm. In view of this translation of myth into reality, it is doubly important that one should consider whether there might not be other myths which suggest factors other than transactions costs as the impetus towards the development of firms. Since the present work is not a treatise on the origin and growth of the firm we do not intend to dwell on this subject at length, but given that the underlying view of the firm that one adopts when analysing overseas investment is of such importance, we do feel obliged to give the matter some attention.

Our choice of Hobbes as an illustration of the 'thought experiment' method of analysis is not entirely accidental, since there does exist an account of the origin of the firm which has some similarity to the analysis of the State presented in *Leviathan*. It was the suggestion of Frank Knight (1921) in *Risk, Uncertainty, and Profit* that the origin of the firm was really a response to the risks which are present in a world of uncertainty.

In a world of free competition, in which all exchanges are conducted in open external markets, it is highly likely that a situation of uncertainty would be the normal state of affairs, with considerable fluctuations in personal incomes. Just as Schumpeter (1943) has characterized a perfectly competitive economy as one of high risk for firms because of the absence of monopoly profits as a cushion against changes in demand, techniques, circumstances, etc., so in the pure exchange economy that we are imagining individuals run the risk of unstable incomes with potential fluctuations between prosperity and want. According to Knight, in such a situation of uncertainty there would be individuals of a particular nature – potential entrepreneurs – who, at the prospect of profits, would be willing to assume the greater share of the economic risks. Firms come into existence because individuals agree to place their work under the control of entrepreneurs in return for a guarantee of stability in the payment for their work. The entrepreneur, in his turn, receives the fluctuating residual income (after payments to the factors) as his reward for bearing the risks of production. In Knight's analysis, therefore, it is the risk-taking entrepreneur who brings the firm into existence with an offer of stability and certainty in the lives of others.

Interesting as it is to speculate upon the nature of the firm, we should not lose sight of the fact that, in all probability, neither of these accounts of the origin of the firm is an accurate description of history. To draw a parallel with Hobbes again, any realistic account of the early rise of government would, for example, have to make due allowance for the possibility that the sovereign was able to dominate others, with the aid of guile or strength, and achieve a position of power which naturally reinforced itself. In a similar manner, in the analysis of the firm one would surely have to recognize that firms as institutions may have evolved in a less than co-operative manner. To take some examples, changes in work organizations may have been forced through by individuals or groups who had a concentration of wealth (Marglin 1978, Francis 1983): some firms may have developed from the early monopolies and patents granted by the monarch; some may have developed from the drive and foresight of particularly gifted men; the motive force, particularly for expansion, may have been the quest for monopoly power (Robinson 1934); and so on.

Since we have not undertaken an historical study of the evolution of firms, and since we do not feel that those studies which have been made (for instance Chandler 1977 and Hannah 1976) shed sufficient light on this subject, we are unable to give an answer to the question of origin. In so far as one must rely upon what we have called myth, however, our own sympathies would lie with an explanation which emphasizes the dynamic problem of risk and uncertainty, the strategies of entrepreneurs and the presence of monopoly (for a few examples see Robinson 1934, Kalecki 1937, Schumpeter 1943, Marris 1972, Littlechild 1981).

After this rather lengthy digression we leave the general question of the development of the firm and turn to some of the specific arguments of the transactions cost approach as they have been applied to overseas investment.

Transactions costs and overseas investment

We have already referred to three principal components of direct investment to which the transactions cost/internalization argument may be applied. For the first of these categories, primary production, it has been argued that, before the war, the growth of international firms was linked with the growth in demand for primary products. Buckley and Casson (1976) argue that because these products are often geographically concentrated and are associated with a volatile supply and price structure (with inadequate futures markets) there was an incentive to internalize their production within the firm, along transactions cost lines, in order to stabilize supply and price. Dunning (1981, p. 32) would seem to concur with this analysis since he suggests that the subsequent externalizing of raw material markets, in the post-war period, illustrates that the net gains of internalization lessened as those markets became less imperfect.

No doubt the development of raw material and food supplies on the scale desired by colonial firms required a heavy investment in modern mining and plantation systems of production, controlled by the firms themselves, since the absence of a capitalist infrastructure, the absence of organized markets and the presence of much 'peasant' production was not conducive to the production of a surplus for export. It is, however, quite another matter to view this process simply as the circumventing of imperfect external markets which make transactions difficult. Given what is known about the development of colonial markets – that, for instance, firms tended to invest largely in the colonies belonging to their own country, and that their control of production was maintained, explicitly and implicitly, with the help of political and military dominance – it is surely straining the market failure analysis beyond any reasonable limits to regard it as the principal explanation of economic development in this period. Similarly, it is surely realistic to view the subsequent 'externalizing' of raw material markets as much more a reflection of emerging economic and political independence, in the post-colonial period, than as a response to changing transactions cost factors.

The second category of overseas direct investment, the establishment of a foreign subsidiary for distribution, is perhaps more amenable to the internalization approach, though here it would seem that the important influences concern strategic factors such as risk-taking and opportunistic behaviour (which have been incorporated into the transactions cost approach by Williamson 1975) rather than the uncertainties of pricing contracts.

If we suppose that the firm initially locates production in its home base, then, typically, when it turns to overseas markets and begins to export it may sell its products via agents in the foreign country in question. The initial reason for this is likely to be that the firm is uncertain of the potential for its product in new territories. It does not wish to commit itself to the heavy fixed costs of establishing distribution outlets, because of the risk of losses if the product is unsuccessful. Of course, the policy chosen will depend upon the dynamism of the entrepreneur and his willingness to take risks, but for the sake of argument, we can take this initial 'sale by agents' as typical. Assuming, however, that the firm's product is successful and market penetration grows, it can be argued that market transactions of this kind (selling by agents) become increasingly difficult to sustain as sales grow and as they become geographically concentrated. Problems arise concerning the sharing of any risk between producer and distributor in holding large inventories, particularly if demand is subject to significant shifts. This, coupled with the possibility that production may require after-sales servicing or adaptation, may make the sales contract increasingly less attractive than a distribution outlet which is part of the firm's own hierarchy. Perhaps of most importance, however, is the difficulty caused by potential conflicts of interest, and the possibilities for opportunistic behaviour on the part of the agents.

While the firm naturally wishes its product to be promoted and serviced to the fullest possible extent, and while negotiations with agents may elicit such a promise, in practice the firm's product may be only one of a range within the agent's portfolio. This implies that the agent may distribute his promotional efforts (and any after-sales contact) across various products so as to maximize his own profits. It is possible, therefore, that the outcome may lead to a selling effort for one firm's product which is considered unsatisfactory from that firm's perspective. Even if there is a choice of alternative agents – and this is not necessarily the case – the possibility that the same problem might repeat itself may lead the firm to establish its own distribution network, which allows it to vary selling intensity, or style, in line with its own corporate strategy.

Since distribution networks must, by their very nature, be located in the country of sale, the implication is that an international firm will be established. This argument in favour of internalization is greatly strengthened by the additional factor of national differences in fiscal arrangements. The establishment of a network of distribution subsidiaries effectively means that the firm sells its products to its own subsidiary, which in turn sells them in its own national market. This implies that, within limits, the firm can adjust its internal pricing arrangements so as to minimize reported profitability in higher tax countries, without necessarily establishing manufacturing units in those countries.

The remaining category of foreign direct investment – manufacturing investment – is our principal concern and is the one to which the transactions cost argument has been most commonly applied. Briefly, the argument is that over the post-war years there has been a tremendous growth in industries which rely heavily upon intangible assets, particularly knowledge derived from research and development expenditure. If it were possible for parties to agree a common price for the worth of these assets, the argument goes, and if each party could rely upon the other to obey the spirit as well as the letter of any contract, it would be possible for the domestic firm to license its intangible asset to an already existing indigenous firm overseas. By doing this, it would gain through the licence the rent associated with the intangible asset without establishing an overseas facility. However, because these intangible assets are, by

41

their nature, difficult to value, it is highly likely that the parties will disagree over their price and will have insufficient trust in each other to allow adaptation and valuation problems to be solved as they arise (Buckley and Casson 1976, Caves 1982). Internalization (and overseas investment) has occurred therefore in those product areas where intangible assets and knowledge have been important, and international firms have been created where the markets to be internalized have cut across the national boundaries.

The first point we should note here is that the transactions cost argument is not in itself sufficient to explain the existence of international manufacturing firms, and must be supplemented by an analysis of locational factors along traditional lines. One line of argument may be that exporting from the firm's domestic base is ruled out because of transport costs, tariff barriers, factor costs differences, etc., so that the firm must choose – along transactions cost minimization lines – between licensing and overseas production (Caves 1982, p. 3). Alternatively, one may suppose that the firm makes the decision whether to internalize production or license overseas and then, if it does internalize, decides on the basis of locational considerations whether to produce overseas or export from the domestic base (Dunning 1980). Whether locational considerations come into play before or after the internalization decision is unimportant in practice; what is important is that even in the framework of the transactions cost approach locational forces are still the prime mover in the decision whether to export or not. Given that the locational considerations are paramount in the export decision, the remaining matter to consider is the choice between licensing and overseas production.

The problems of pricing and trading intangible assets are undoubtedly factors which increase the difficulty of establishing licensing agreements and hence promote the establishment of foreign manufacturing facilities. What we can consider now, however, is whether there are other important motives for controlling overseas production which do not rely upon transactions problems as such.

As a general point we should bear in mind that in many instances, although it may be possible to place a reasonably precise value on the firm's operations, licensing may not be a consideration if the comparative advantage is not readily separable from the firm itself – if, for instance, it is the ability of the management, derived from experience in the market, which enables it to co-ordinate an efficient production and selling operation with a standardized product. As we move away from this position, and allow for identifiable and separable know-how, designs, processes, and so on, there may be further obstacles to licensing as a form of market servicing.

First, the choice between licensing and overseas production may depend upon the motivations of the owners and managers of the firm and,

42

even if licensing yields an equivalent rent to overseas production, the firm may choose overseas production if it is motivated by desires other than profit. For example, if the firm is a sales maximizer, or if the management gains satisfaction from being part of a large international organization, then overseas investment may be favoured over licensing. While the influence of entrepreneurial motivation may be important in some cases, it seems likely, however, that other considerations are of more general significance.

If we take it, for the sake of argument, that the potential rent derivable from the firm's production advantage is given and agreed by all interested parties, the overseas production decision will depend upon the nature of the competition which the firm faces in overseas markets and the risks of investment. In most licensing cases the firm would almost certainly in practice be negotiating with a foreign company which possessed some monopoly power of its own. This need not lead to small numbers exchange problems, but it does suggest that in order to take up a licence the foreign firm would require a share of the rent which was at least (and probably more than) sufficient to compensate it for the profits it could have gained from using its energies elsewhere. This would, therefore, reduce the rent available to the firm which holds the comparative advantage and hence would, other things being equal, promote overseas investment rather than licensing.

Whether the firm does in fact set up overseas production will depend upon how it views the nature of the competitive environment, together with its attitude to risk. By going alone overseas, the domestic firm has the possibility of greater profits, by gaining all of the monopoly rent in question, but against this it must balance the risks of competition from existing foreign firms, who may be prepared to suffer short-term losses in an attempt to prevent the new entrant from securing a strong position in the market. In establishing overseas production, the firm therefore risks reducing its monopoly rent to a level which is below the share it would have gained from licensed co-operative production.

One cannot indicate a priori in which direction the firm's decision will go, but it is possible to say a little more about the factors influencing the risk analysis implicit in the investment decision. First, one would expect, other things being equal, that the greater the required investment, relative to the firm's total capitalization, the greater would be the incentive to license production, because of the potential danger to the firm's overall wealth and liquidity positions should the overseas venture fail (Kalecki 1937). Put another way, the larger the firm, the more able it is to absorb the increased marginal risk which stems from heavy investment, and so the more likely it is to take on the risks of overseas production.

Second, the risks involved in overseas investment are, as we have said, dependent upon the nature of the competition the firm faces. On the one hand, the greater is overseas competition the greater are the risks of losses in production. On the other hand, this is balanced by the possibility that foreign competitors, if they have or can develop potentially similar product lines or techniques, may be unwilling to pay more than a nominal royalty payment in negotiating the licence. The final decision between overseas production and licensing may, therefore, be a finely balanced one which depends on the attitude of the entrepreneur to risk-taking. While this is a rather general conclusion, what one can perhaps suggest is that larger firms are more likely to undertake overseas investment, partly because they have a greater capacity to face success- fully a competitive struggle with foreign firms, and (more tentatively) because their size may be an indication of their willingness in the past to bear the risks implied by the growth process overseas. This said, one is of course likely to find differences in strategy between firms of similar size and in related situations: those businesses which are managed by risk-takers are more likely to engage in overseas investment than those which prefer certain profits with minimum risk.

Once we allow for the presence of competitive uncertainty and risk, it is clear that these have a pervasive influence on the firm's general investment and production strategy. It is tempting to limit the considera- tion of uncertainty to a specific investment plan, but in practice one investment often cannot be separated from the firm's general growth. When a firm engages in an activity, it is not confronted with a fixed 'blueprint' of possibilities which arise from that activity; one direction may open up other avenues of activity which were previously unknown at the time of the investment (Littlechild 1981). If natural growth in the life of the firm does arise in part from a diversity of experience in production, this provides an incentive for the firm to maintain control of its activities in a variety of markets, both as a potential source of future growth and as a denial to competitors of the benefits of learning by doing.

We have followed the drift of the market failure approach in discussing those monopolistic advantages that the firm possesses which, though they may be intangible, are nevertheless identifiable. It should be recognized, however, that the firm's competitive strengths may lie elsewhere. While it is common in static analysis to identify well-defined monopolistic traits as the explanation of 'above-normal' profits, in reality this perhaps gives insufficient emphasis to the entrepreneurial function. In a dynamic economy, some firms do not have a monopolistic advantage as such, but possess the ability to 'create or notice profitable opportunities that are, in principle, available to anyone' (Littlechild 1981). In such cases, the question of licensing does not arise, but the possibility does exist for the firm to apply these abilities in overseas production.

Finally, it is important to note, once again, that there is a qualitative difference between establishing a new overseas venture and the expan- sion of an already existing subsidiary. The presence of an established overseas subsidiary suggests that the risks connected with further investment, the threat of foreign competition, etc., are significantly less than they would be for a firm which was establishing itself in a new environment. Because of the experience and know-how of the overseas management the subsidiary is akin to a foreign firm. The implication is that one would expect licensing ventures to be less prevalent among firms who, previously in their history, had already made a commitment to overseas production.

In summary, we would suggest that considerations such as those we have discussed imply that licensing may, on average, be less profitable than internal production and less beneficial to the overall interests of the firm. Particularly when the firm is large, and when it already has an overseas presence, the firm itself would tend to choose overseas production if exporting were ruled out by locational considerations. The difficulties of pricing and trading intangible assets may be an additional cause of overseas investment, but, in so far as these assets are proxied by such measures as research and development and advertising intensity, this may be a reflection of the tendency of large and dynamic firms to engage in such expenditures (cf. Taylor and Silberston 1973) rather than a reflection of transactions cost difficulties as such.

III Some macroeconomic considerations

So far our discussion has concentrated on the characteristics of individual firms. In this section we examine whether there are any general macroeconomic considerations which might affect the overseas investment strategies of firms as a whole, within a particular country.

There are various explanations of the UK's traditional position as an exporter of capital during the late nineteenth and early twentieth centuries which rely upon what might be classified as general macroeconomic factors (see for instance Edelstein 1982). These explanations emphasize both 'push factors' emanating in the UK – such as Hobsbawm's over-saving thesis, or the notion that domestic rates of return had declined as industrialization proceeded – and 'pull factors' emanating from overseas – for instance, the high rates of return on infrastructure investment in the 'New World'. Generally, however, these factors are mainly relevant to an explanation of portfolio investment, which was indeed the form that most British investment overseas took during the period. In the case of product manufacture, high rates of return (or profits) may not account for direct investment overseas since, other things being equal, these returns might in principle be obtained from exporting.

The same general statement can be applied to other macroeconomic explanations of why firms are attracted abroad, which rely upon the existence of a large, fast-growing, foreign market, perhaps coupled with a slow-growing, depressed, domestic market. In the absence of any qualification, market size and growth arguments explain only why a firm may be attracted to the overseas market, and do not indicate why it should not meet this demand from an export base. Indeed, if anything, the existence of a depressed home market provides a good reason why the firm should increase its export endeavours, in order to make full use of existing domestic capacity. Neglecting straightforward cost differences and the like, arguments which rely upon market prosperity in themselves only suggest direct investment overseas if they imply some additional external benefits associated with an overseas location for production. The major external benefits which come to mind are those connected with having a production or major distribution centre in a prosperous market in which new products and designs, new organizational structures, and new production and selling techniques are developed more quickly than in the firm's domestic market. An intimate association with these markets, as opposed to an 'arm's-length' association via exporting, may provide 'spill-over' benefits to the firm which improve its ability to service other markets, both domestic and foreign. To the extent that this has any significance, it has probably been of most importance in attracting firms to the United States, which traditionally has been, and in many ways still is, a leader in the development of new products and selling techniques.

The importance of currency differences

The next point to consider in this section is whether the existence of differing national currencies has any bearing on the overseas investment decision. The most well known theory, in this context, is Aliber's (1970, 1971) 'currency premium' analysis.

Aliber suggests that foreign direct investment can best be explained by imperfections in capital markets, rather than by factors associated with the firm itself. He argues that international firms may exist because they have an advantage in the capital market which enables them to value a given income stream more highly than a firm based in a foreign (host) country. The essence of this advantage is that the international firm, by virtue of being based in a country with a 'strong' currency, may be able to borrow at a lower rate of interest, or have its earnings capitalized at a higher rate, than the host-country firm. Behind this advantage lies the attitude of investors to exchange rate risk.

It is argued that investors require a premium to compensate for the existence of uncertainty about future exchange rate changes, so that they will require a 'currency premium' on any debt denominated in a 'risky' currency. For instance, if the US dollar is considered to be a 'hard' currency, relative to sterling, then the rate of interest on debts denominated in sterling will be higher than on debts denominated in dollars. Likewise, the rate of capitalization applied to an income stream denominated in dollars will be higher than on an income stream which is identical in all respects, save that it is denominated in sterling. The final step in Aliber's argument is to suppose that because investors are ignorant about the proportion of the international firm's earnings which arises overseas, they tend to apply the parent country capitalization rate to the whole of its earnings. It follows that if the currency premium on dollars is less than the currency premium on sterling, the rate of interest on the debts of the US firm will be lower than the same debts of a UK firm, and the rate of capitalization of its income stream will be higher. The implication therefore is that the US firm can undertake operations identical to that of the UK firm, and yet be more profitable: it is this which gives the US firm its advantage in competition.

While admitting that the currency premium argument is an interesting possibility, most commentators have tended to disregard it. This is, in part, because the theory does not appear to explain the significant amount of cross-investment between countries and because overseas investment continues from countries even after their currencies no longer appear to be strong. While the latter point could perhaps be explained in terms of further investment taking place to strengthen and build upon previous investments, in general the currency premium argument is difficult to reconcile with observed investment flows.

One way of viewing the importance of currency instability might not be as an isolated consideration, but as part of the general stability of the country which is being considered as a location for the firm's investment. When making this decision, the firm will be influenced by the political stability of the country, whether it suffers from balance of payments problems which might lead to restrictions on dividend flows, whether it has a co-operative, stable work force, and so on. One part of this 'basket' of stability factors might be the stability of the currency because of its implications for recorded profits, capital gains and losses, etc., in the firm's balance sheet. We would suggest, however, that the influence of different national currencies may not come from strength or weakness in the currency as such – which in Aliber's terms means whether it is stable or subject to fluctuations and hence whether it attracts a risk premium – but from the possibility that currencies may be under- or over-valued for lengthy periods of time.

It is not an uncommon, if by no means a unanimous view, that during the inter-war years and parts of the earlier post-Second World War years, sterling was over-valued and that in the 1950s and the 1960s the same was true of the dollar. At the same time, during the 1950s and 1960s, it is argued that certain economies – particularly Germany and Japan – had currencies which were under-valued. Part of the reason given for this is that the United Kingdom and the United States, because of their importance in the world economy during the times in question, acted as international bankers, and were allowed to run significant deficits because other countries were anxious to acquire their currencies for use as an international trading medium. In addition, in the case of the under-valued currencies, it is often argued that there is an asymmetrical pressure on exchange rates, in the sense that there is less pressure on a surplus country to revalue than there is on a deficit country to devalue, since the former can merely accumulate reserves at the existing exchange rate.

The credence which is placed upon this interpretation depends on how one views the operation and evolution of the international monetary system, and, in particular upon which theoretical approach to balance of payments adjustments one finds most realistic (for instance, the monetary approach to the balance of payments would be less sympathetic to the views considered). We do not intend to involve ourselves here in a discussion of the merits of alternative views of the balance of payments, and the relationship between the current and capital accounts. Suffice it to say that the views we have referred to are common enough to make it worth considering further the potential influence of currency over-valuation. The easiest way to approach the question is to consider the impact of a devaluation.

The traditional approach to devaluation is that devaluation works, if it does, by changing the relative price of exports abroad and imports at home. If the usual Marshall–Lerner conditions hold – and there are unused resources available to switch to exporting and import substitution – then a devaluation will improve the trade balance in the short run. For the trade balance to be improved in the long run it is necessary to suppose that increased import costs do not lead to wage and price rises which offset the relative price improvements induced by the devaluation. Alternatively, even if quantity responses are low, firms may use the devaluation to increase (or restore) profit margins to satisfactory levels (see Posner and Steer 1979, for an elaboration of these and other points).

Allowing that devaluation has the traditional effects described, it can be argued that it will also affect the profitability of overseas production. For instance, if we consider a British firm with operations in Germany, then with costs and prices set in Deutschmarks, overseas German profits are unaffected by the devaluation of sterling – they are determined by the German price–cost margin and the level of output. Given these German profits, however, the impact of a sterling devaluation is to raise the firm's profits in sterling terms. In the case of exports to Germany, if we suppose that prices are set in marks, and costs (in the UK) are set in sterling, then the first round impact of devaluation is to raise prices in sterling terms (the mark price is fixed), while leaving sterling costs unchanged.

Assuming, for simplicity, that the quantity of exports is not changed, it should be obvious that the devaluation raises sterling export profits by a greater proportion than it raises overseas production profits. Of course, in practice, there will be some increase in UK sterling costs to the extent that increased import costs feed through to UK money wages and prices. However, for the devaluation not to lead to a switch in relative profitability in favour of exports, it would require domestic average costs to rise by the same percentage as the initial devaluation.

What we can argue is that if devaluation does work along traditional lines, then it induces a shift in relative sterling profitability in favour of exporting, as against overseas production. Since this is, in effect, equivalent to shifting relative production costs between countries in favour of the UK, it is likely to lead, other things being equal, to an increase in export servicing of foreign markets relative to overseas production. If unemployment is relatively high, so that there are unused resources available to switch to exporting (and the pressure on money wages to rise is reduced), then devaluation is more likely to succeed and hence the change in the relative profitability of exporting and overseas production is the more likely.

In so far as devaluation is often considered to be a short-term (or possibly medium-term) policy instrument, one would not expect it to have a very significant impact on the overseas production–export choice. This choice is presumably based on long-run considerations of relative profitability and would be influenced by currency valuations only if their effect was considered pseudo-permanent, so that they had a lasting impact on relative costs between countries. In practical terms, this is just what is implied by the view that sterling and the dollar were over-valued for long periods. Granted this, and given that re-valuation works in the opposite direction to devaluation, the implication is that conditions in the United Kingdom and the United States were, during the periods in question, more conducive to overseas production than to exporting. This is not to suggest that this was the most important factor, but that, given the other determinants of the location decision, countries with an over-valued currency would be more inclined to favour overseas investment. In the case of countries with under-valued currencies, the reverse would be true.

Tariffs and trade restrictions

The final influence we include in this section is that of tariffs and other forms of trade restrictions. Their impact is quite straightforward, in that selective tariffs and import quotas serve either to raise the price of exported commodities, or restrict their quantity, and so provide an additional inducement to direct investment. While in principle the firm could, faced with trade restrictions, divert its energies to producing non-restricted goods, in practice the specific investments which it has in current lines of production, both in human and physical terms, make it most efficient to attempt to hold on to existing lines of production. This suggests a strong impetus to overseas investment.

How important trading restrictions are as a general explanation of foreign direct investment clearly depends upon the size of tariffs, the length of time they are in operation, and the range of goods to which they apply. For the moment, we leave this point with two observations. First, the world economy has been characterized by very definite phases when tariff barriers have been generally prominent. Tariffs were particularly high and extensive during the late nineteenth and early twentieth centuries, and during the inter-war years: both of these periods contained years of depression when trading restrictions were introduced in an attempt to alleviate import competition. Second, although the post-Second World War period is often characterized as a period of freer trade (with formal international agreements) there have still been significant tariff barriers in the world economy. In addition, in so far as informal trading restrictions have become so important – partly because of nationalistic buying policies, particularly on the part of governments, and the introduction of administrative and other restrictions against exports – it has become more difficult to judge what the true situation regarding free trade has been (see P. D. Henderson's Clare Group article, *Midland Bank Review*, Winter 1983).

IV   The development of international firms

In this section we briefly draw together the main elements of our discussion in order to highlight those factors which require consideration in subsequent chapters. The implication of what has been said so far is that to understand the current pattern of overseas direct investment it is necessary to examine the development of international firms. Accepting that the overseas investment behaviour of the firm is merely a part of its more general strategy for supplying overseas markets, this suggests a number of aspects of the firm's development which are of particular importance.

First, the significance we have attached to previous marketing and investment decisions implies that the firm's general historical development is important. It is a truism to say that the firm is a product of its history since current production decisions inevitably involve the use of capital, know-how and labour which were accumulated or developed in an earlier period. In a more fundamental sense this recognition forces us to view the current form of the firm as the product of an historical evolution within a unique economic and political environment. While it is often convenient in economic analysis to abstract from such matters, our discussion indicates that this is a consideration which is of great importance to an understanding of overseas investment. To give this matter proper attention would, strictly speaking, require a thorough examination of the evolution of individual firms. Although we have not attempted such a study, we do briefly consider in the next chapter, as a second-best alternative, some international aspects of the development of the British economy, to give at least a background picture of the early development of British international firms.

Second, whichever of the approaches to overseas investment one considers most suitable, it is clear that there is common agreement in emphasizing the importance of locational forces in the choice between overseas investment and exporting as alternative means of market servicing. There are several possible locational influences, ranging from factor cost differences to political buying restrictions. It is important to identify which have been significant in practice, because although in principle they all have the same effect – to promote overseas investment – each has a different implication for the domestic economy. To take one example, if overseas investment has been stimulated at the expense of exports by factor cost differences between the UK and overseas, then it might be possible, in theory at least, to counter this tendency with an appropriate policy of devaluation and wage restraint in the domestic economy. If, on the other hand, overseas investment is principally a response to tariff restrictions, then such a policy would be ineffective, since any circumvention of the existing barrier by domestic price changes would presumably be countered with a further increase in overseas tariffs in order to maintain the initial objective of reduced imports.

The final question which must be considered concerns the decision to control production within the firm rather than to license to overseas manufacturers. We have suggested that the decision to produce overseas rather than license may be a reflection of the interplay of risk and competition, and the greater benefits for potential profitability and growth which may evolve from the control of production. Having said this, however, it is extremely difficult to differentiate competing explanations of overseas investment since much of the evidence which is available from statistical sources is compatible with more than one explanation. To take the example we gave in an earlier section, the tendency of firms which invest overseas to engage in above-average amounts of research and development expenditure may be one indication of the presence of intangible assets which are difficult to license, but it may also be a reflection of the competitive strength of large firms which have the ability to bear the risks of expanding via overseas production.

As we have already suggested in the preliminary remarks of the first chapter, these and similar questions suggest the need for a relatively

51

detailed examination of the firm's strategy, which pays regard to the potential differences between industries and between products within industries. The later chapters of the book attempt to provide this detail by considering the overseas investment behaviour of a sample of inter-national companies. First, however, we turn to the general historical background to British foreign investment.

CHAPTER FOUR

Historical developments in overseas investment

It was suggested in the previous chapter that an understanding of the current pattern of overseas manufacturing investment requires some understanding of the historical development of that investment. In the present chapter we attempt to do this, by examining the origins of overseas manufacturing and then considering its subsequent growth in relation to the broader changes which have taken place in the domestic economy. This discussion serves two purposes: it assists our understanding of the nature and causes of overseas manufacturing investment, by placing such investment in the context of general British economic development and, at the same time, it provides a link between the earlier theoretical discussion and the detailed case study material which follows.

I Trade, protection and overseas investment

It is possible to argue that once overseas manufacturing investment reaches a certain critical point, a significant part of that investment subsequently grows under its own momentum, in the sense that decisions to produce overseas may have involved such heavy physical and human investment that subsequent market growth is naturally serviced by an extension of the existing overseas facility. Whatever the merits of this view, it is certainly the case that the early growth of British manufacturing investment overseas was intimately, and principally, connected with the development of Britain's trading position in the world economy. More specifically, any analysis of Britain's overseas direct investment position must begin with developments in international trade in the nineteenth and early twentieth centuries.

In the decades leading up to the establishment of free trade in the mid-nineteenth century, and for several decades after this, Britain could with justification claim to be the world's leading industrial nation and the major force in world trade. Some figures for the period 1856–1913 illustrate this.

British exports, as a percentage of GDP, rose from 14.6 per cent in 1856 to 18.3 per cent in 1873 and 25 per cent in 1913 (Matthews *et al.* 1982, p. 433). In 1870, when the UK's relative lead over other countries was perhaps at its peak, the total foreign trade of the United Kingdom was greater than the combined totals of Germany, France and Italy (Ensor 1936, p. 104). Similarly, the structure of trade reflected Britain's industrial strength. In 1860 over 90 per cent of Britain's total imports were of raw materials and foodstuffs. Although this proportion gradually declined over the years, in 1913 raw materials and foodstuffs still accounted for just over 80 per cent of imports. Conversely, in 1860 over 85 per cent of home produced exports were of finished manufactures. While this proportion also declined up to the First World War, in 1913 the figure was still in the region of 75 per cent (Schlote 1952). These trading figures are even more impressive if one considers the UK's share of total world exports of manufactures: over the period 1881–5 this share stood at no less than 45 per cent, and, despite the decline which followed, in 1913 the UK was still supplying almost 32 per cent of world exports of manufactures.

Britain's importance to the world economy during these years is also reflected in the figures for her capital exports, which again were substantially greater than those of other countries. For instance, British net foreign investment abroad was in the region of 5 per cent of GDP per annum between 1870 and 1913, as opposed to less than 3 per cent for France and less than 2 per cent for Germany. In 1913, the accumulated stock of net foreign assets stood at 180 per cent of GDP (Matthews *et al.* 1982, p. 128). It would appear that the majority of these assets (in the region of 70 per cent) were of a portfolio kind directed to government bond issues, railway building and other infrastructure projects, while the remaining direct investments were connected with raw material extraction and plantations. Given this structure, it is not surprising that the most important recipient countries were the 'newer' expanding countries and those with colonial ties – principally the USA, Canada, India and Ceylon, South Africa, Australia, Argentina and Brazil (Edelstein 1982, p. 40).

Given the UK's competitive strength in international markets in the nineteenth century, and the relative absence of trade barriers, it is understandable that to begin with there was little overseas direct investment in manufacturing, with Britain traditionally taking the role of an exporter of manufactured products. This situation began to change, however, as the end of the nineteenth century witnessed a movement to protection, in part as a response to the developing manufacturing interests of other countries, and in part as an attempt to protect domestic markets following the downturn in economic activity which occurred in this period. While in the UK the only duties which were retained were those designed to raise revenue rather than protect domestic industries –

the duties on tea, tobacco, wines, etc. – in Europe and the USA general tariff levels gradually rose through the late nineteenth and early twentieth centuries until they stood at, for instance, 33 per cent in the USA and Spain, 18 per cent in France, 17 per cent in Italy and 12 per cent in Germany (Lewis 1949, p. 48). In particular, while in 1914 there were no tariffs on industrial products in the UK, these stood at, for example, 41 per cent in Spain, 20 per cent in France, 18 per cent in Italy and 13 per cent in Germany (Pollard 1981, p. 259). Even in the Dominion countries there was a movement towards protection. Although British goods enjoyed preferential treatment over others, the tariffs against UK manufactures were significant, and on some goods higher than those that British manufacturers faced in Europe (Abel 1945, Benham 1941).

In a country such as the UK, where firms traditionally had a heavy dependence on international markets, one would expect the introduction of trading restrictions to provide two responses: a search for newer, less restricted markets, and greater emphasis on domestic markets. The former response certainly occurred. Increasingly British exports became directed away from industrial Europe and the USA, towards the less industrialized regions (particularly Asia and Africa) where competition was less severe and where, in many countries, Empire association assisted market penetration (Hobsbawm 1969, chapter 7, Schlote 1952). No doubt British firms also increased their endeavours in domestic markets but here there was perhaps less scope for expansion because of already large market shares and the absence of tariff protection of a kind enjoyed by firms overseas.

For an efficient and dynamic firm which is faced with trade barriers, an additional response is to set up production behind the barriers, and this is just what British firms did: they attempted to hold on to foreign markets which had been built up through exports. We have already noted that the imposition of tariffs was an important cause of the shift in the pattern of British exports away from industrialized areas and towards less developed countries. At the same time as this occurred, it would seem that British firms began to establish manufacturing facilities in those same industrial areas.

Although there is little direct statistical evidence available, we can get some indication of the direction of this early foreign manufacturing investment. The evidence provided by Stopford (1974, 1976) from a sample of British companies suggests that the greater part of overseas manufacturing investment before 1914 was directed towards the industrialized countries of Europe, the USA and the developed Commonwealth: the countries which had imposed substantial tariffs against British manufactures. Houston and Dunning (1976) have identified those companies which by 1914 had production facilities in at least four countries. Excluding primary activities, the majority of these firms were located in the traditional sectors of textiles, mechanical engineering, metal goods, household goods, and food and tobacco. Notable examples include, in textiles, J. & P. Coats, Courtaulds, and English Sewing Cotton; in engineering, Vickers, S. Pearson & Son, and Minerals Separation; and in household goods, etc., Lever Brothers, Reckitts, and Liebigs. Of the companies which did begin to manufacture overseas before the First World War, it is not surprising that most were among the then largest British companies (Hannah 1976, pp. 120–1) and were significant suppliers of exports to overseas markets.

Although the late nineteenth and early twentieth centuries witnessed the beginnings of overseas manufacturing by British firms, the first period of real expansion occurred in the inter-war years. Again it seems that the most important single factor in promoting overseas investment was the growth of tariff restrictions (Chandler 1980). Without going into the details of trade developments in the inter-war years, it is well known that the late 1920s and 1930s witnessed a phase of prolonged and severe recession in the world economy, and the response of all industrial countries was to raise tariffs and other forms of trade restrictions in order to protect domestic markets. British companies, like others, received protection in domestic markets in a series of measures (such as the Safeguarding of Industries Act and the Import Duties Act) introduced between 1925 and 1932 (Abel 1945). For our purposes, however, it was the raising of tariffs overseas which is of the greatest interest.

In the USA and Europe, general tariff levels rose dramatically through the inter-war years and, by the early 1930s, tariffs in many countries were more than double the already high level of 1913 (Pollard 1981, pp. 299–303). At the same time as this occurred, British trade was severely hampered in the older developed Commonwealth countries. UK manufacturers had received some preference over non-Empire producers since before the First World War, but this preference usually took the form of a percentage reduction of the tariff on 'foreign' products, with the result that because the absolute level of tariffs was high, UK manufacturers still faced substantial barriers. While there were political efforts to promote an increase in Empire trade (culminating in the 'Ottawa agreements' of 1932) by a system of cross-preferences between the UK and the Dominions, the results were generally a further increase in tariffs. The Ottawa agreements were designed to restrict foreign imports which were in competition with products the Empire could supply, but in practice preferences for UK manufacturers were usually given by raising the tariff on non-Empire products rather than by reducing those on British goods. In many instances, where British firms were in competition with developing indigenous manufacturers, little or no preference was granted. To give a typical example, in Australia the tariffs on woollen piece goods, clothing, and machinery stood respectively at 65, 50 and 50 per cent for foreign manufacturers, while UK firms faced tariffs on the same goods of 45, 35 and 45 per cent (Benham 1941).

Partly on account of these tariff measures, the level of British exports to the USA, Europe and the Old Commonwealth declined substantially. Within this reduced total, however, the presence of some Imperial preference did promote a shift in the share of British exports going to the Empire – the percentage rose from just over 43 in 1930 to 50 in 1938 (Schlote 1952, Benham 1941, McDougall and Hutt 1954). In parallel with this development in trade, British firms turned to overseas manufacture as a way of retaining market shares. The difference from the pre-First World War period, however, was that the decline in export markets and the stimulus to overseas production was on a much greater scale.

Overseas manufacturing investment continued in Europe and the USA during the inter-war years but the most important destination in this period was the developed Commonwealth (Stopford 1976). While Imperial preference had induced some shift in (the reduced levels of) exports to the Commonwealth, it is not surprising that there was a tendency for overseas manufacturing investment to move to the same areas. In so far as there existed a limit to the degree of capital expansion which British firms could safely undertake overseas, given their size and resources, it was natural that a preference should lie with the Commonwealth countries. This preference no doubt reflected the close political and cultural ties which made overseas investment in these areas a less risky affair than investment elsewhere. Markets were more familiar and the political climate of the host countries was considered more favourable than that of countries which had no ties with the UK.

There is a scarcity of statistical evidence on overseas investment in the period, but again one can get some indication from the growing list of firms which established overseas production facilities. In addition to the previous examples, such companies as Distillers, Metal Box, GKN, ICI, Rowntree, British Oxygen, Babcock & Wilcox and Renold Chains were added to the list of international firms in existence by 1938 (Houston and Dunning 1976). It is not surprising that the majority of companies which moved into overseas manufacture were from the list of large British firms of the period (Hannah 1976), who could bear the costs and risks of overseas expansion and who already had a vested interest in overseas markets.

It seems to be undoubtedly the case that, for all areas, the major stimulus to much overseas manufacturing investment of the period were the obstacles imposed on export markets. Apart from the strong implication suggested by the behaviour of tariffs and exports, some of the important company histories covering the period confirm this view. While in particular instances such factors as transport costs and the advantages of being close to the market were significant, the factor of most general importance seems to have been the imposition of, or threat of, trade restrictions (see, for example, Wilson 1954, Ward-Jackson 1941, Tripp 1956). In the absence of direct evidence, however, it is often as well to rely upon the judgement of contemporary observers such as R. M. Kindersley. Kindersley had undertaken regular annual surveys of Britain's overseas investments. In his survey, published in 1939, just after the outbreak of hostilities with Germany – in a special issue of the *Economic Journal* which assessed Britain's war potential – he explained manufacturing investment by noting that,

> owing to the growth of tariffs and other forms of economic nationalism since 1929, the obstacles to trade have become so numerous that many British companies have found it more convenient to establish subsidiaries and branches in foreign countries for the manufacture of finished products, rather than to export the finished products themselves.

Before we leave the inter-war years, there is one other influence on the relationship between export performance and overseas production which we should consider. Although practically all industrial countries suffered a set-back in their export performance between the wars, the decline was particularly significant for UK firms. In the first place, because the UK had such a large share of world exports of manufactures, the absolute impact of declining export markets was particularly severe for British firms. Discounting this absolute effect, however, the UK suffered to a greater extent in export markets than many industrial countries in relative terms also. Between 1913 and 1937 the UK's share of world exports of manufactures declined from almost 32 to nearer 22 per cent. To an extent, this decline was a natural reflection of the rise of other industrial countries and the consequent reduction in the share of world output accounted for by the UK economy. However, the change also reflected a relative decline in the export performance of British firms during the inter-war years. For example, using 1929 as a base of 100, there was a fall in the export/output ratio in UK manufacturing industry from 132 in 1913 to 59 in 1937, compared to an overall fall from 107 to 82 for other industrial countries over the same period (Matthews *et al.* 1982, pp. 435–6). This relative decline is part of a more general trend which has extended through the post-war years and no doubt has a variety of explanations. In the inter-war period, however, the decline was particularly pronounced and may be in part due to a factor which certainly influences the overseas investment decisions of firms, the influence of the exchange rate.

We discussed in the previous chapter the impact upon the overseas investment decision of an over-valued exchange rate. It was suggested that over-valuation implies that domestic costs are high relative to overseas costs and this tends, other things being equal, to promote overseas production at the expense of exports. Because profit margins on exports are smaller than they would be at a lower exchange rate, the firm is less able to absorb transport costs, tariffs, etc., and hence is more inclined towards overseas production.

It was certainly a common view at the time that the exchange rate in the 1920s and early 1930s was too high and was damaging the export performance of British firms, particularly after the return in 1925 to the old pre-war parity of $4.38. Roughly, the argument is that even before the First World War the UK had continued to run a deficit on the balance of trade, indicating that the prices of UK manufactures were, to a degree, uncompetitive in world markets. A fall in the exchange rate was avoided, however, because the deficit was offset by the substantial property income which came from abroad (derived from portfolio investment) and by relatively small interest rate changes which induced short-term capital movements, because sterling was the major international currency. These deficits persisted after the First World War, and sterling was finally taken off the gold standard in 1931, in response to growing unemployment in the staple export industries and a growing deficit in the trade balance which was increasingly difficult to finance because of a much reduced inflow of capital from abroad (Benham 1941). While it is a debatable point whether there could have been a substantial and effective devaluation of sterling in the 1920s – particularly in view of the likelihood of retaliation (see Matthews *et al.* 1982, pp. 470–3) – it nevertheless remains true that British exports did appear to suffer from a price disadvantage in foreign markets which must, at the margin, have strengthened any inducement to undertake overseas production from other motives.

II   Post-war developments

While the experience of the inter-war years provides a partial explanation for the beginnings of large-scale foreign direct investment by British manufacturing firms, some of the trends established during this period stimulated the early post-war growth of foreign direct investment. To begin with, the establishment of manufacturing facilities in the USA and Europe, and particularly in the developed countries of the Commonwealth, contributed to a change in what might be called the 'environment' of the overseas market servicing decision. Even after the dilution of trade restrictions (and it is as well to remember here that in many instances formal trade restrictions were still significant in the 1940s and 1950s) it was to be expected that a certain amount of natural growth in overseas investment would occur as markets expanded, since already existing production and distribution networks provided, for some products, a bias which favoured this form of expansion. In addition, British firms had already gained valuable experience in the operation of overseas production and in the dealings in capital markets necessary to finance this expansion, and this must have reduced, at the margin, the perceived risks of overseas investment.

Perhaps the most important 'spill-over' from the inter-war years, however, was that the relative shift in export markets to less developed countries established a potential trend towards direct investment as those countries gained greater economic and political independence. Some of the products which were being exported were just those that were liable to face trading restrictions as countries developed their own industrialization programmes after the war. Although the General Agreement on Tariffs and Trade, signed in 1948, was intended to liberalize trade generally, less developed countries imposed relatively high quotas and tariffs, and the 1940s and 1950s in particular saw a period of planned import substitution in many developing countries in an attempt to encourage domestic manufacturing (see Little 1982 for general developments in post-war trade policy). Since British exports had moved significantly towards these developing countries (in 1951, for example, over 37 per cent of British exports went to developing countries) it is clear that British firms faced an impetus, because of trade barriers, towards overseas production in the kind of standardized products which developing countries wished to produce.

There are no accurate statistics giving the geographical distribution of overseas manufacturing investment during this period, but we can get some idea of the distribution from the samples of firms studied by Reddaway (1968) and Stopford (1976). For a spread of fifteen important countries, both developed and underdeveloped, the distribution of overseas assets for Reddaway's sample suggests that at the end of 1955 roughly 45 per cent of assets were located in the developed Commonwealth and 25 per cent in developing countries. Apart from the usual sampling limitations, these figures may be misleading in so far as they include assets established before the war, and cover some investment in mining which may bias the figure towards less developed countries. It is useful therefore to look at the figures given by Stopford (1976) for new manufacturing investments. The distribution of new manufacturing investments made by a sample of eighty-three British firms implies that over the period 1940–9 some 63 per cent by value were located in the developed Commonwealth, while 25 per cent were located in developing countries. For the period 1950–9, some 43 per cent went to the developed Commonwealth while 37 per cent went to developing countries. Clearly, these figures give some support to the view that investment continued in the important markets of the developed Commonwealth, coupled with import-substituting investment in developing countries in the early post-war years.

Historical developments in overseas investment

Finally, with regard to the period from the 1960s onwards, we have already seen, in chapter 2, that the main change in the destination of overseas direct investment involved a relative movement away from investment in the developing countries and towards investment in Western Europe and the USA, while investment in the developed Commonwealth shows a much greater degree of stability, in terms of percentage of total investment. Although some of the reasons for these developments are discussed in our case study chapters, at this juncture we can note how the trends in overseas investment compare with those of exports. Table 4.1 compares the share of UK outward direct investment by main world area with similar shares for exports, for four selected years.

Table 4.1 UK outward direct investment and exports by world area

Percentages of total net assets (A) and exports (X)					
		1962	*1971*	*1978*	*1981*
Western Europe	A	13.4	21.9	31.0	23.2
	X	40.2	44.4	51.0	53.8
North America	A	23.1	22.0	26.1	34.6
	X	14.3	15.9	12.0	14.0
Other Developed	A	27.1	29.8	23.1	20.4
	X	13.3	11.7	6.6	5.8
Rest of the World	A	36.5	26.3	19.8	21.8
	X	32.2	27.9	30.4	26.4

Sources: Chapter 2, Table 2.3; *Annual Abstract of Statistics*, various years.

The figures in Table 4.1 suggest a few brief comments. First, although direct investment in the developing countries (essentially the Rest of the World in Table 4.1) has declined relatively over the 1960s and 1970s, the percentage of exports has declined by rather less, still accounting for over a quarter of the total in 1981. The majority of the decline in the share of exports to developing countries took place in the 1950s and early 1960s (declining from 37 per cent in 1951 to less than 30 per cent in 1964) and since then the total has been much more stable. This suggests that while developing country markets have continued to be important, the stimulus to overseas production has weakened because of the reduced importance, in the 1960s and 1970s, of import substitution investments,

61

and the relative decline in the importance of the extractive industries. Second, the substantial fall in export shares to the 'other developed countries' (Australia, New Zealand, South Africa and Japan) and the relatively steady figure for overseas investment suggests that, increasingly, market growth in these areas (essentially the developed Commonwealth, excluding Canada) has been serviced by overseas production rather than exports. Finally, the remaining figures suggest that the most important overseas markets for British firms over the period, both in terms of exports and overseas production, have been the high income markets of North America and Western Europe. Having pointed out these trends, however, it is difficult to say much more using the aggregate figures alone, and we leave discussion of causation to our case study chapters.

III Changes in domestic economic structure

The remaining matter which we should briefly consider is the extent to which changes in the industrial structure of overseas manufacturing investment reflect changes in the structure of the domestic economy. We can probably take it that in the early days of overseas manufacturing the structure of that investment reflected the then prevailing strengths of the British economy. For example, the majority of international firms were concentrated, as we have already noted, in the food, drink and tobacco, textiles, mechanical engineering, and metal manufacturing sectors. These sectors were by far the most important for the domestic economy (and for exports) at the time, and this would seem to indicate that overseas manufacturing investment essentially took the form of a simple transposition overseas, in response to trade restrictions, of the then prevailing domestic economic structure. To take 1924 as an example, manufacturing output comprised almost 30 per cent of British GDP, and, within this total, food, drink and tobacco accounted for 16.2 per cent, textiles for 27.3 per cent and mechanical engineering and metal manufacture for almost 14 per cent (Feinstein 1972).

We have already seen that UK manufacturing investment overseas has displayed a substantial shift towards investment in the richer developed countries, particularly in Europe and the USA. Within this total there have been significant shifts in industrial composition, as Table 4.2 shows. The most important trends have been a relative movement away from overseas investment in the traditional areas of food, drink and tobacco, metal manufacture, and textiles, and towards the 'newer' industries of chemicals, electrical engineering and, to a degree, mechanical engineering. It is interesting to compare these changes with those in the domestic economy, in order to see whether the structure of overseas manufacturing has developed independently or in line with domestic

Table 4.2   Sectoral distribution of UK overseas assets in manufacturing

Industry	% of total net assets at end of			
	1954	*1964*	*1978*	*1981*
Chemicals, etc.	11.9	14.2	24.4	28.0
Electrical engineering	5.4	4.9	9.9	10.0
Mechanical engineering, etc.	1.9	1.5	5.8	6.3
Vehicles, etc.	7.9	9.2	2.5	3.4
Food, drink and tobacco	47.3	39.0	27.4	27.1
Textiles, etc.	8.1	6.9	5.1	4.3
Metal manufacture	7.3	9.7	4.4	2.0
Paper, etc.	5.4	8.7	6.9	5.5
Other manufacturing	4.7	5.6	13.5	13.4
Total	100.0	100.0	100.0	100.0

Sources: Reddaway *et al.* (1968); HMSO (1981, 1984), *Census of Overseas Assets* 1978, 1981.

Note: See chapter 2, Table 2.5 for a discussion of the comparability of sources.

industrial structure. If domestic production and exports have moved towards these advanced sectors also, then the developing expertise of firms, and the close relationship between overseas production and trade, would suggest a similar move in the structure of overseas assets. Table 4.3 shows the change in the structure of UK manufacturing industry for representative years between 1930 and 1981.

Table 4.3 suggests that some of the movements in the structure of overseas assets have been accompanied by similar changes in the structure of the domestic economy though on a much less pronounced scale. Textiles and metal manufacture show a relative decline both overseas and in UK production, while chemicals and electrical engineering have shown the largest increase in both. The major anomaly would appear to be the relatively steady share of food, drink and tobacco in UK output (and the steady share of this sector – usually between 6 and 7 per cent – in total UK exports) compared with the large relative decline in the importance of this sector overseas. It would appear that the fast growth of overseas manufacturing in food, drink and tobacco by UK firms in the inter-war and early post-war period gradually declined as the markets matured, and faster growth in the chemicals and electrical engineering sectors gradually reduced the relative importance of food, drink and tobacco. Unlike textiles, however, which continued to decline in importance at home and overseas throughout the period, the food, drink

Table 4.3 Net output by UK manufacturing industry (percentage of total)

Industry	Year				
	1930	1954	1963	1978	1981
Chemicals	5.3	7.6	8.8	9.7	12.0
Electrical engineering	4.3	7.0	8.8	9.1	10.3
Mechanical engineering	8.0	13.1	13.2	14.9	14.0
Vehicles, etc.	12.2	13.1	13.0	11.6	11.2
Food, drink, tobacco	17.6	10.6	11.9	13.0	14.5
Textiles, etc.	20.6	15.3	11.4	8.0	6.7
Metal	5.9	8.5	7.7	5.7	4.7
Paper, etc.	9.2	7.1	7.8	8.4	9.4
Other manufacturing	16.8	17.5	17.3	18.4	17.2
Total	100.0	100.0	100.0	100.0	100.0

Sources: *Business Monitor* PA1002, 1984; *Historical Record of the Census of Production,* London, HMSO, 1978.

and tobacco sector experienced a domestic rate of growth in the 1960s and 1970s which was roughly the average for the economy (see Matthews *et al.* 1982, pp. 240–1 for sectoral differences in growth rates).

The faster-growing sectors, electrical engineering and chemicals, have also experienced an increase in export shares. For example, taking the period 1971 to 1981, the share of total exports coming from these sectors rose from 7.1 to 12.3 per cent and 13.3 to 20.3 per cent respectively. In the case of imports, also, not only have the developed countries, and particularly Europe, increased in importance as a source, but there has also been an increase in the share of imports accounted for by the advanced industrial sectors. To take the same examples, the share of electrical engineering in total UK imports increased from 7.1 per cent in 1971 to 12.3 per cent in 1981, while for chemicals the increase was from 11.9 to 15.5 per cent.

The figures we have presented can be regarded as giving an indication of a change in the structure of the British economy (and British firms) towards increased integration with advanced industrial markets over the post-war period. Within this, however, it is possible that the greater growth of overseas manufacturing in the more technologically intensive sectors, relative to their domestic growth, is an indication of a relative failure, compared with other advanced countries, in the growth and export performance of the UK economy. For example, Dunning (1979) and Panic (1982) suggest that, although British firms have been internationally competitive (in the sense that they possess what Dunning calls ownership advantages), the UK has, because of its slow rate of growth (which is also a manifestation of other problems), become an unattractive location for the production of new and sophisticated products. This has tended to push UK firms into overseas production and, at the same time, to encourage foreign firms to export high technology products to the UK. The implication is that, if this continues, the UK will increasingly be left with lower value-added, less sophisticated, production.

The question of whether UK international firms are tending to produce high technology, high value-added products overseas is one which we shall consider, to some degree, in our case study chapters. As a preliminary to this, however, it is helpful to look at the matter in slightly greater detail. Taking the 1970s as an illustrative period, Table 4.4 below shows the trade performance of the major industrial sectors of the UK economy for the years 1970 and 1978, where those sectors are split into so-called high technology and low technology sectors (see chapter 2 for

Table 4.4 Trade balance by industry

Industry	Trade balance (%)		Change in trade balance
	1970	1978	(1978 − 1970)
Chemicals	+6	+9	+3
Mechanical engineering and Instrument engineering	+14	+13	−1
Electrical engineering	+5	+3	−2
Rubber	+13	+8	−5
Vehicles	+14	+5	−9
*Food, drink and tobacco	−15	−10	+5
*Textiles, etc.	+2	−5	−7
*Paper, etc.	−12	−9	+3
*Metal manufacture	+1	−1	−2
*Other	−2	−2	0

Source: Calculations from *Economic Trends*, 1980, vol. 320.

Notes: (a) Trade balance = Exports minus imports/home demand plus exports.
   (b) Positive sign indicates a positive trade balance or a positive gain. Negative sign indicates an adverse balance or change.
   (c) Asterisk indicates less technologically intensive sector.

details). The trade balance ratios in the first two columns show the balance of exports minus imports for each sector as a percentage of home demand plus exports (see Wells and Imber 1977 for details of this and other measures of trade performance). The third column of Table 4.4 shows the change in the trade balance over the period (the ratio in 1978 minus the ratio in 1970).

Table 4.4 shows that the trade balance has generally been positive in the technologically intensive sectors and negative in the less technologically intensive sectors, particularly food, drink and tobacco. However, as column three shows, over the 1970s there was, with the exception of chemicals, a deterioration in the trade balance in the 'advanced' sectors. Conversely, in the less technologically intensive sectors the trade balance over the 1970s showed rather less deterioration, and in some cases a marked improvement.

At first sight, Table 4.4 would appear to give some support to the notion that recent trends in overseas manufacturing investment have reflected (or caused) an adverse change in the structure of trade, along the lines suggested by Panic (1982). While this may be the case, we should, however, be careful in interpreting these relatively aggregative figures. For instance, if we look more closely at one of the technologically advanced sectors – electrical engineering – which increased its share of overseas manufacturing investment and suffered an adverse change in its trade balance, the picture becomes less clear. Although it is generally correct to regard the electrical engineering industry as a research and development intensive sector, within the industry there is considerable variation between, for example, domestic appliances, which are relatively standardized products, and radar equipment which is sophisticated. Table 4.5 shows the same changes in the trade balance when the electrical engineering sector is disaggregated. Figures for research and development expenditure for each sub-sector are unavailable, but the table does include value-added per man as a very rough alternative indicator of sophistication in the industry.

An examination of Table 4.5 indicates that within the overall adverse movement of the trade balance for electrical engineering there is considerable variation. Roughly speaking, the greatest deterioration in the overall trade balance comes from those relatively unsophisticated parts of the sector – particularly domestic electrical appliances and broadcast receiving equipment – where value added per man is lowest (and where research and development expenditure as a percentage of net output is also lowest). In the more advanced areas, such as electrical machinery and radar and electronic capital goods, there was a small improvement in the trade balance over the period.

One possibility which suggests itself is that, within the electrical engineering sector, it is the relatively unsophisticated products which

Table 4.5 Trade balance and value-added in electrical engineering

Industry	Trade balance ratio		Change	Value-added per man
	1970	1978	1978–1970	£
Electrical machinery	+14	+25	+11	6,804
Insulated wires and cables	+14	+22	+8	6,962
Telegraph and radio apparatus	+10	+7	−3	6,044
Radio and electronic components	−2	−2	0	5,724
Broadcast receiving equipment	−6	−20	−14	3,620
Electronic computers	−14	−13	+1	16,733
Radio, radar and electronic capital goods	+13	+15	+2	7,342
Domestic electrical appliances	+8	−6	−14	4,978
Other electrical	+9	+7	−2	6,117
Total	+5	+3	−2	6,608

Sources: See Table 4.4, and *Business Monitor* PA 1002, 1984.

Note: See Table 4.4.

have contributed to a large part of the increase in overseas investment in the sector, while the technologically advanced products have sustained their overall export performance. We would not wish to push the argument further at this stage, since there are great difficulties of interpretation, particularly as there are so many possible influences on trade performance. What we would stress, however, is that this sort of exercise confirms what we suggested in our preliminary remarks of chapter 1: to understand recent movements in overseas manufacturing investment it is necessary to examine in some detail the behaviour of individual firms within overall industrial sectors.

IV   Summary

We have suggested that the early growth in British manufacturing investment overseas was largely a response to the development of trade restrictions in the world economy during the inter-war years. These restrictions were particularly important for the UK manufacturing sector because of its heavy reliance on export markets. The result was that a number of large firms in the traditional sectors of the British economy began to manufacture overseas in an attempt to hold on to overseas markets. The development of overseas manufacturing in the post-war period was influenced by three important factors. First, the location and industrial composition of the early overseas manufacturing investments made it likely that the post-war years would see some growth in the traditional sectors, particularly in the Commonwealth, as these investments expanded with natural market growth. Second, overseas investment in the developing countries increased in the early post-war years, following the previous orientation of British exports to these markets before the war. As developing countries imposed trade restrictions to encourage indigenous manufacture, this induced a further expansion in overseas investment in the traditional industrial sectors which were being built up.

Finally, the post-war development of UK overseas investment reflects the orientation of British trade (and the British economy) towards advanced industrial markets and technologically intensive industries. Although the early development of overseas manufacturing in, particularly, textiles, metals, food, drink and tobacco, has meant that these sectors still account for a significant share of UK overseas assets, increasingly the emphasis has shifted towards the chemical, electrical and mechanical engineering sectors. Although a similar change has occurred in the domestic economy, the relative movement in overseas assets has been much more pronounced and has coincided, recently, with a worsening of the trade balance in these sectors.

CHAPTER FIVE

The sample of firms

The previous chapters have examined the general trends in UK direct investment overseas. In the case studies which follow, we attempt to provide a more detailed understanding of developments in overseas manufacturing investments by examining the experience of a sample of individual companies. Before these studies are presented, however, we should discuss briefly the selection of our company sample and assess how representative it is of UK industry as a whole.

I The composition of the sample

We were concerned to construct a sample of companies which could in some way be described as representative of UK industry. Obviously this would involve choosing companies from as wide a range of industrial sectors as possible. The question thus arose as to whether this choice could be made on scientific grounds, perhaps using weights derived from aggregate statistical data.

Taking 1978 as an appropriate example year, a sectoral breakdown of overseas assets (analysed by the industry of the UK enterprise) reveals that almost 75 per cent of the book value of UK direct investment was attributable to manufacturing industry (HMSO 1981, pp. 16–17). Of these assets attributable to manufacturing firms, 80 per cent were in manufacturing facilities and 16.2 per cent in distribution facilities. This clearly suggests that any sample of UK companies chosen for detailed study should favour the representation of manufacturing enterprises. Furthermore, the most prevalent criticism of overseas direct investment is perhaps its alleged export displacement effect, and manufacturing industry typically accounts for over 80 per cent of total UK exports of goods. We have therefore limited our sample largely to manufacturing firms, although we have also included two conglomerates with manufacturing interests, for the experience of their subsidiaries.

Within manufacturing industry (see Table 5.1) the most active sector was Food, drink and tobacco, which accounted for 28.6 per cent of total assets invested abroad by UK manufacturing industry in 1978. Next in

69

Table 5.1 Sectoral distribution of UK outward direct investment by manufacturing industry at end of 1978 (excluding oil companies, banks and insurance companies)

Industry of UK enterprise	Percentage of total book value of net assets at end of 1978
Food, drink and tobacco	28.6
Chemicals and allied industries	19.1
Metal manufacture	2.4
Mechanical and instrument engineering	13.2
Electrical engineering	10.4
Shipbuilding	0.5
Motor vehicles	1.9
Textiles, leather, clothing and footwear	3.9
Paper, printing and publishing	5.9
Rubber	2.4
Other manufacturing	11.8
Total	100.0
Total (£ million)	14,350.7

Source: *Census of Overseas Assets 1978*, Business Monitor MA4, 1978 Supplement, London, HMSO, 1981, pp. 16–17.

Note: Compare with Table 2.5 where analysis is according to the industry of the overseas affiliate.

importance came Chemicals (19.1 per cent), Mechanical and instrument engineering (13.2 per cent), Other manufacturing (11.8 per cent) and Electrical engineering (10.4 per cent). At the other end of the scale Shipbuilding, Motor vehicles, Metal manufacture and Rubber together accounted for only 7.2 per cent of the total.

The above analysis provides a guide to the selection of a sample of companies for detailed study, but it is only a guide. Any purportedly 'scientific' sample based on precise weights derived from the statistics would be as spurious as it would be difficult to construct. Many, if not most, international enterprises are active in more than one industrial sector. The firms who are asked to respond to the Department of Trade inquiry on overseas assets are allowed either to report on a group basis or to provide a separate return for each UK subsidiary. In the latter case, each UK subsidiary would be classified according to its main UK activity. In the former, all the overseas assets of the group would be classified according to its largest UK industrial activity, but this might account for less than half the group's total activities. There is therefore an element of approximation in the published statistics which makes it impossible to state categorically that all the assets allocated to a particular sector are necessarily engaged in activity in that sector. Moreover, the Department of Trade is not prepared, for reasons of confidentiality, to divulge either the overseas investment stake or the industrial classification of any particular firm or group. There is thus no way of knowing how assets of any one group have been allocated among the various industrial sectors.

The above discussion suggests the problems involved in trying to construct a cross-sectional sample of firms using precise weights derived from the overseas investment statistics. Such considerations not-withstanding, it is still possible to construct a reasonably representative sample according to an approximate categorization of particular firms. Twenty-three (out of a total of forty-six firms contacted) agreed to participate in our study. The firms are listed below, but where a company has preferred to remain anonymous we have referred to it simply as Company A, B or C. The industrial classification shown is tentative, for the reasons cited above, and reflects the information with which the companies provided us.

Food, drink and tobacco	Cadbury-Schweppes; Rothmans International; United Biscuits
Chemicals and allied industries	BP (British Petroleum) Chemicals[1]; Glaxo; The Wellcome Foundation; Company A
Mechanical and instrument engineering	Davy Corporation; Smiths Industries; Tube Investments; Guest Keen & Nettlefolds; Company B; Company C; Ferranti; Racal; Thorn EMI
Shipbuilding and motor vehicles	AE (Associated Engineering)
Textiles, leather, clothing and footwear	Coats Patons

[1] The oil company, BP, has been categorized according to the activities of the manufacturing subsidiary.

71

Paper, printing and publishing	Reed International
Other manufacturing (including metal manufacture)	Foseco Minsep; Metal Box; Pilkington; RMC (Ready-Mix Concrete)

In constructing this sample, we attempted to obtain a spread across manufacturing industry, while giving particular weight to those types of company whose experiences are most instructive with regard to the motivation behind recent overseas direct investment decisions. Hence (see the case studies in chapter 7 for further details) we chose to study rather more engineering firms than food, drink and tobacco companies, although many of the companies – e.g. GKN – embrace more than one sector.

A number of other considerations should also be borne in mind. First, the response to our enquiry was of course voluntary. Of the companies contacted, half did not take up our invitation to participate. The main reason cited for refusal was that the executives were hard-pressed and did not have the time to answer our questions. This means that there is an element of self-selection in our sample. Critics of our study might say that this introduces an element of bias towards those firms who had 'nothing to hide'. Second, all our firms are large. The motivation behind the decisions of small firms to invest abroad may well differ in certain respects.

Last, and perhaps most significant, the manufacturing sectors identified in the published statistics from which we have drawn our sample are so highly aggregated that there is almost as much diversity within each grouping as there is between them. For instance, 'Chemicals and allied industries' embraces Orders IV and V of the Standard Industrial Classification (revised 1968) and includes twelve Minimum List Headings. The choice of a sample of companies to represent the whole sector was clearly an impossible task. It is, for example, highly unlikely that the factors governing overseas investment by firms in the pharmaceutical industry are identical, or even particularly similar, to those governing overseas investment by firms who manufacture bulk chemicals. On a related topic, we drew attention in chapter 2 to Dunning's classification of industrial sectors into more or less technologically intensive, on the basis of their R & D expenditure as a percentage of net output. To take the example of Mechanical and instrument engineering in 1978, at one extreme, firms who manufacture scientific instruments and systems spent 2.92 per cent of their net output on research and development. At the other, companies who fabricate industrial plant and steelwork spent only 0.78 per cent. Yet both belong to the same aggregate sector which has been termed 'more technologically intensive' under Dunning's classification. The 'industrial plant and steelwork' industry, however, spent less on research and development than many industries which are classified as 'less technologically intensive' – e.g. food, drink and tobacco.

It follows from this that there is no way in which any sample could be chosen which could be said to be truly representative of all the firms in a particular sector, let alone all the firms in the UK manufacturing industry. Yet we need not be reduced to considering each firm as a special case. Points of similarity do emerge between diverse companies in any given industrial sector, and some general conclusions can be stated with reasonable confidence. It is these areas of similar experience which we highlight in our discussion of the case studies in chapters 6, 7 and 8.

II The coverage of the sample

As we have explained, the Department of Trade is not prepared to divulge data on the book values of net assets overseas of individual companies. We are thus not able to derive any direct measure of the coverage of our sample in relation to total UK overseas direct investment. We can, however, provide some illustrative data on net assets employed, turnover and trading profits for our companies (see Table 5.2) for 1980. Figures for the anonymous companies are not revealed individually, but are included, approximately, in the totals.

Not surprisingly, BP is by far the largest. The other twenty-two manufacturing companies have a combined total of net assets employed of approximately £12,000 million, turnover in the region of £22,000 million and trading profits of about £1700 million. These figures may be compared with (provisional) data published by the Government Statistical Service which show that net assets employed in all UK manufacturing industry in 1980 were £76,860 million, and profits generated were £8957 million. Our sample thus represents about 15 per cent of UK manufacturing industry, assessed on the basis of net assets employed, and almost 19 per cent in terms of total trading profits in manufacture. Such proportions indicate that the coverage of our sample as regards domestic manufacturing industry is comparatively small. However, as overseas direct investment is typically carried out by large companies, we might expect that a rather larger proportion of total UK overseas assets would be attributable to the sample.

Indeed, many of the companies appear to generate a large proportion of their turnover overseas. The data in Table 5.3 show the proportion of total Group sales to outside customers generated by subsidiaries and branches located overseas. At one extreme, Rothmans International produce 90 per cent of their sales overseas. Pilkington, Coats Patons, The Wellcome Foundation, Davy and Foseco Minsep all produce more than 50 per cent. At the other extreme, Ferranti – which is also the

Table 5.2 Size distribution of company sample in terms of net assets employed, turnover and trading profit[1] in 1980

	Net assets employed (£m)	Turnover (£m)	Trading profit (£m)
BP[2]	12,843	20,374	2,510
Company A	–	–	–
Pilkington	1,088	786	45
GKN	962	1,922	62
Thorn EMI	779	2,228	125
Reed	689	1,480	55
Rothmans[3]	652	964	84
TI	527	1,158	49
Glaxo	442	710	84
Cadbury-Schweppes	427	1,118	80
Coats Patons	410	689	66
United Biscuits	367	880	55
Company B	–	–	–
Wellcome	338	442	42
Company C	–	–	–
Racal	294	533	88
Metal Box	288	1,076	52
AE	206	441	19
Davy Corporation	146	670	13
Smiths Industries	143	319	30
RMC	124	735	51
Foseco Minsep	122	264	23
Ferranti	100	271	20
Total (excluding BP)	12,000	22,000	1,700
All manufacturing industry	76,860	–	8,957

Source: Company reports; *Company Finance* Business Monitor MA3 Fourteenth issue, London, HMSO, 1983, p. 5.

Notes: 1 The figures relate to companies' accounting years ending closest to 31 December 1980. Net assets employed are defined as fixed assets, goodwill, investments and net current assets, including short-term bank loans and overdrafts. Trading profit is defined as profit before the deduction of interest on loans and before crediting the share of profits of associated companies and other income from investments. Turnover is defined as sales, net of sales taxes, to third parties – i.e. excluding intra-Group sales.

2 Trading profit is after deduction of petroleum revenue tax and other production taxes.

3 Turnover is after deducting value added taxes, tobacco duties and all other sales taxes.

Table 5.3 Geographical analysis of turnover, trading profit and employment of company sample, 1980[1] (excluding anonymous companies)

	Percentage of total relating to overseas operations		
	Turnover[2]	Trading profit[3]	Employment
BP	58	73	65
Pilkington	58	125[4]	49
GKN	35	149[4]	36
Thorn EMI	32	27	n.a.
Reed	22	50	29
Rothmans	90	n.a.[5]	n.a.
TI	29	n.a.	n.a.
Glaxo	31	n.a.	n.a.
Cadbury-Schweppes	38	39	33
Coats Patons	64	79	66
United Biscuits	33	32	24
Wellcome	61	n.a.	n.a.
Racal	37	n.a.	n.a.
Metal Box	41	84	34
AE	30	42	25
Davy Corporation	55	n.a.	52
Smiths Industries	25	24	n.a.
RMC	48	45	n.a.
Foseco Minsep	74	n.a.	n.a.
Ferranti	3	n.a.	2

Source: Company reports.

Notes: 1 Definitions of turnover and trading profit are as given in Table 5.2. Employment is defined as the average number of persons employed during the year.

2 By source – i.e. according to the country of production. Some companies only provide a breakdown of turnover by point of final sale. In such cases, the figures entered in the table above are derived using data on UK exports and assuming no Group imports into the UK. Some companies only provide a geographical analysis of turnover which includes intra-Group sales.

3 Some companies did not provide a geographical breakdown of trading profit but of some other measure (e.g. profit before tax). In such cases, the analysis above uses these figures.

4 Figure exceeds 100 per cent because negative profits were earned in the United Kingdom.

5 n.a. = not available.

smallest company in the sample – manufacture 97 per cent of their products in the United Kingdom. The relative size of different companies, and the different degrees to which they manufacture overseas should be borne in mind when interpreting the results in chapter 6. In analysing the qualitative information from our interviews and questionnaires, we will assess the significance of particular answers on the basis of the number of companies responding. Ferranti thus has equal weight with Rothmans, or BP. Yet, as we have seen, the difference in the scale of their overseas activities is large.

As regards UK and overseas profits, the sample data provide few interesting results. The recession in the United Kingdom in 1980 obviously had its effect on some of the companies, particularly Pilkington, GKN and Metal Box. Profit margins in the UK seem overall to be slightly lower than overseas, and this affects the comparisons, but too much reliance should not be placed on one year's figures. Finally, we provide data on employment. Again, it is difficult to make any firm statements, but it appears (from comparing the first column with the last one) that turnover per employee is similar both at home and overseas.

III The company interviews and the questionnaire

Having discussed the composition of our sample of companies, we turn next to a consideration of the usefulness and reliability of the qualitative information which we obtained from the companies.

Our initial contact with any company was through a letter to the Chairman asking for co-operation in our study. If the response was positive, we would typically be invited to talk to one or more members of senior management. In these meetings, we would try to elicit three types of information. First, we would attempt to establish a straightforward historical record of the development of the company concerned, particularly with regard to its servicing of overseas markets and its establishment of overseas production facilities. We would thus ask largely factual questions about the timing of overseas investments, what products were manufactured overseas and how the markets had previously been serviced. The answers, as one might expect given the factual nature of the questions, were largely uncontentious and could in many cases be checked independently.

We would then turn to a series of questions about the organization, control and finance of overseas affiliates. For example, we were interested in ascertaining how much autonomy is given to overseas affiliates with regard to their pricing/marketing/investment decisions. We would also ask whether overseas direct investment was usually financed by funds transferred from the United Kingdom or whether foreign currency borrowing and/or local equity participation were preferred alternatives. The answers to these questions were generally not clear cut. The meaningful distinction turned out not to be that between complete independence and full control, but between different degrees of autonomy. Similarly, finance does not usually come wholly from UK funds or from local funds but partly from each source.

The questions in the last group were much more conjectural, and were concerned with an evaluation of overseas direct investment. We thus needed some idea of what would have happened in a hypothetical alternative position if the overseas investment had not been undertaken. Answers to these hypothetical questions were difficult both for executives to provide and for us to validate independently. If a manager maintained that domestic production and export was not an alternative because overseas customers insisted on local supply, the only way to check the assertion would have been to ask the overseas customers. Such a course of action was beyond the scope of our study. Unfortunately, it is precisely these 'uncheckable' answers that we would most like to be able to verify. A major criticism levelled at overseas direct investment is, as we have pointed out, its alleged export displacement effect. It would be unduly optimistic on our part to expect company executives to admit readily to a corporate strategy which has had adverse effects on domestic employment. In practice, our main check on the validity of responses was provided by the answers of similar companies, our general knowledge of overseas investment by firms in many countries, and our intuitive understanding, developed through the study, of what seemed reasonable.

Our contact with senior managers was often extended to a second or third meeting, particularly if the company in question was engaged in many diverse overseas activities. After the final interview, we would leave a questionnaire covering most of the important issues outlined above, which we would ask the company to complete. These questionnaires, together with records of our meetings, form the basis of the analysis in the chapters that follow.

CHAPTER SIX

Why do firms manufacture overseas?
Some preliminary evidence

We have discussed, in earlier chapters, the importance of barriers to trade as a stimulus to direct investment overseas. It was suggested that during the inter-war and earlier post-Second World War years, the most significant historical factor in the growth of overseas manufacturing investment was the attempt by firms to hold on to and expand in foreign markets which were previously supplied from exporting, and which were subsequently restricted by tariffs and other barriers to trade.

When one considers the general trend in the location of British manufacturing investment overseas, it is apparent, as we have already seen, that over the post-war years there has been an increasing relative movement away from direct investment in Old Commonwealth and developing countries, and towards advanced industrial economies, especially Western Europe and the United States. While there are obvious dangers in attempting to pinpoint a precise period during which significant changes in the location in overseas investment occurred, we have suggested that such a change happened, roughly, from the 1960s onwards.

In the analysis of individual firms, which we present in this chapter, it has been necessary to make some judgement of how to limit both the period of time and the range of countries which we cover (and the number of firms to be included in the sample). We have discussed, in chapter 5, the problems which are involved in composing a sample which can be considered broadly representative and in obtaining information which can be considered reliable.

At this point we summarize again an important principle which has guided us in our choice. First, since we have already attempted an explanation of a significant proportion of overseas investment in the inter-war and early post-war years, we give this period less attention here. Second, because of the important change in geographical destination referred to above, we have decided to concentrate on direct investment in Western Europe and the United States, covering mainly the period 1965–80. In restricting ourselves to this later period we have, in addition, implicitly recognized that any attempt to cover periods much earlier than this would be severely hampered by the fading memories of those who took the investment decisions (even if they are still with the firm), and the lack of documented evidence. Concentrating on the later period has the advantage that the relevant people are still likely to be with the firm, or that the basis of the decisions is still widely appreciated among those who subsequently succeeded them. We should emphasize again, however, that since investment decisions are part of an evolving strategy, one cannot in practice avoid discussing earlier periods and making comparisons with investments in countries outside our strict area of interest.

I   Servicing foreign markets

It is helpful at this stage if we recall the framework suggested by the traditional theories of overseas investment, since our questionnaire to the firms was constructed largely with this in mind.

We can take it that if a firm is considering the possibility of supplying overseas markets it must possess two characteristics. First, it has, or believes it has, a competitive advantage which would enable it to gain some share in foreign markets. Second, it has sufficient dynamism, and is sufficiently motivated by potential profits, to enter or expand in these markets. The firm's advantage may come from the demand side of the market, in that it has a product which, to a greater or lesser degree, is considered desirable by the purchasers. The product may be unique, and may face little competition, or it may have characteristics that are considered (marginally) more desirable than the products of other firms. Alternatively, the firm's advantage may come from the supply side, implying for instance that the firm feels that because of its managerial expertise and experience, or its access to better techniques and processes, it has (abstracting from locational considerations) an edge over the competition.

When deciding whether to meet overseas demand from an export or overseas base, the firm must also consider whether it should attempt to license production to firms which already have a presence in the markets in question. In many instances, this choice will be easily made, or not even considered, since the competitive advantage may be based upon such factors as experience, know-how, faith, minor differences in product specification, selling expertise, risk-taking, an early awareness of a potential demand, and so on, which are not readily saleable to an outside party. On the other hand, if the advantage is more clearly defined – based, say, on distinctive designs, processes, or specialist knowledge – then the firm's decision is a more difficult one. Abstracting from the

80

important possibility that the entrepreneur may – for reasons of personal identification with the firm – have a strong preference to retain production within the firm, the crucial considerations are the method by which the firm feels it can best extract the monopoly rent which is associated with its acquired advantage, and the implications of licensing for the firm's long-run competitive position. Since we have discussed, in chapter 3, the factors which might affect this decision, we need not repeat the arguments here, and merely note that there is a strong presumption that, in the majority of instances, the firm would be unlikely to extract the full monopoly rent through licensing and hence would be more inclined to undertake production itself. This is particularly likely when the firm is large enough to bear the risks of overseas production, or when it has an already existing overseas subsidiary.

Assuming that the firm has decided to undertake production itself, the final decision which it must make is whether to locate production in its domestic base or overseas. If the estimated size of the overseas market is limited, then it is likely that the firm will initially supply it by making more intensive use of its existing capacity, perhaps with minor additions. Alternatively, although the estimated market size might be significant, the firm may be sufficiently risk-averse to wish to test the market initially by exporting. The initial decision will in part be determined by the firm's previous experience with overseas production. If it already has existing subsidiaries located overseas, its greater familiarity with foreign conditions may imply that uncertainty will be less significant.

Whatever the initial considerations, after the firm's policy is given a practical test, it may be necessary for it to reconsider its production strategy. If the market has proved sufficiently attractive, the firm may well wish to increase its overseas presence. This may lead it to establish its own marketing and distribution subsidiary (replacing sales by agents), so that it can develop a co-ordinated and sustained sales effort. In conjunction with this, or after further success in the market, the firm may consider whether it is desirable to establish an overseas manufacturing facility.

If the firm already has a strong overseas presence then the decision to move production overseas may be easier to make, since it is more akin to the extension of an already familiar operation. This apart, however, one could argue that, for early investments at least, there is a strong locational inertia, favouring a domestic location, which has to be overcome – an inertia based not only on the preferences of the managers, but also on the presence in the domestic market of human and physical investments in existing production and managerial systems. The decision which is finally made may involve an all-or-nothing choice – because, for instance, trading barriers of various kinds, transportation costs or low-cost competition make it impossible to compete in the long run from an export base – or a marginal choice, based for example on transport costs or lower overseas costs, which is centred around relative profit comparisons between alternative locations.

We should mention at this point that there is another explanation for the decision to move overseas if this involves the acquisition of an existing overseas firm. Such an acquisition may enable the firm to acquire additional products or technologies which complement and improve the firm's existing domestic operations. The acquisition may therefore improve the performance and profitability of the domestic firm by an amount greater than the value which is placed upon the overseas firm when considered in isolation. Following the take-over, the firm might review the possibilities of a change in location, but, given the locational inertia connected with the existing overseas operation, it is highly likely that the overseas facility would be retained for some time at least.

To summarize, we have a number of factors which influence the firm's overseas selling strategy, involving the way it perceives its production advantages, its ability to bear risk, the attraction of overseas markets, and various locational considerations. While these perceptions are no doubt influenced by unique considerations which stem from the nature of the owners or managers of the firm – their attitude towards expansion and to risk-taking, their foresight and so on – the most important factors are likely to be those determined by the nature of industries in which the firms are placed, the nature of their products, and the nature of the competitive environment. We shall consider individual firms in detail in the next chapter, but to begin with it is helpful if we consider the range of responses to some of our general questions.

II Questionnaire responses

In this section we report the responses to selected questions which were put to the firms in the form of a questionnaire. These questions relate to the nature of the firm's competitive advantages in production, its attraction to overseas markets, and its decision to move to overseas production rather than licensing or exporting. We consider responses both to direct questions concerning the firm's motives, and to indirect questions concerning the nature of its products and the competition it faces. While this sort of approach has difficulties, essentially because of the great diversity of experience among firms and the fact that many produce several products, it nevertheless provides a useful general background which can be qualified and expanded when we consider the individual firms in detail.

Production advantages and overseas attractions

We began by asking firms how they perceived any advantages which gave them some competitive strength in overseas markets, whether serviced by exports or overseas production. The firms were given a range of examples to choose from and encouraged to mention other alternatives. Table 6.1 summarizes the responses.

The answers to the question in Table 6.1 were not particularly surprising, in that the most important factors were seen as entrepreneurial (related directly to the quality of the firm's management) or connected with the quality of its product, often based upon technological advantage. The only surprising factor, at first sight, is the low weight attached to brand loyalty or advertising, particularly since product differentiation is a commonly stressed explanation of competitive advantage in the

Table 6.1 What do you think are the main advantages that your company (or product) possesses which enable it to compete with foreign or indigenous firms overseas?

		No. of respondents = 23	
	Examples	*No. of firms mentioning*	*% of respondents*
1	Special management expertise	10	43
2	Quality or design of product	16	69
3	Patent restrictions	6	26
4	Brand loyalty or advertising	3	13
5	Technological lead over competitors	10	43
6	Integration of operations in the UK or elsewhere	4	17
7	Tax allowances or other incentives	0	–
8	Other (see note)	1	–

Note: Market control, combined with good marketing and reasonably good technical back-up.

83

overseas investment literature. This does not necessarily imply that product differentiation is unimportant, but that, if it is, the firms see it as connected more with the actual quality of the product rather than with advertising or customer loyalty. An additional point to mention is that a significant proportion of overseas sales is of intermediate products, rather than products for final consumption, and one would expect tangible quality and design factors to be given greater emphasis here than brand loyalty as such. It is interesting that the firms which did refer to brand loyalty were situated in the food, drink and tobacco industries, serving the final consumer directly.

Given that the firm possesses some production advantage, the next point to consider is why they were attracted to the supply of overseas markets. The responses are summarized in Table 6.2.

Table 6.2   What factors attracted your company to the overseas market?

	Examples	No. of firms mentioning	% of respondents
		No. of respondents = 23	
1	Market size	20	87
2	Market growth	9	39
3	Absence of competition	1	–
4	Stagnant domestic market	1	–
5	Other (see note)	4	17

Note: Other factors mentioned were (a) limit of growth reached in UK, (b) the ending of previous cartel agreement with competitors, (c) technical changes in the United States which favoured the company's existing product, (d) defence against European competitors entering the UK market.

Again, the emphasis upon market size and market growth – which are difficult in practice to separate – is not surprising, and accords with previous studies of US firms which emphasize these factors (see for instance Dunning 1973). Most of the firms in our sample are large and an important aspect of their strategy is a desire for further expansion. It is interesting, however, that only one firm mentioned a stagnant, or depressed, UK market as a stimulus. This does not mean that domestic market conditions are unimportant. A number of firms told us, during the interviews, that they had achieved a large market share in the UK and that overseas sales were thus increasingly attractive. This implies that it is limitations on further expansion, rather than depressed conditions as such, which make overseas sales a relevant consideration. While there do exist domestic routes through which firms can, and do, expand – particularly through product diversification – accumulated experience and know-how in existing product areas make overseas sales a particularly attractive route, since they build upon existing competitive strengths.

Finally, of the other factors mentioned, two refer to responses to the behaviour of competitors, while the remaining one refers to a firm in the motor accessory industry where experience in European markets left it well-placed to service the US car market as the market moved to smaller cars, following the rise in oil prices in the mid-1970s.

Overseas production

At this point we turn to the important consideration of why firms chose to service the overseas market by overseas production. Before we give the reasons for this, however, Table 6.3 outlines the manner in which markets had been serviced before overseas investment was undertaken.

Table 6.3 Before production facilities were established in Country X, how was the market serviced?

	Examples	No. of respondents = 20	
		No. of firms mentioning	% of respondents
1	Not produced in X	7	35
2	Imported from UK	12	60
3	Produced under licence in X	1	–

Although Table 6.3 largely speaks for itself, we should say that it needs to be interpreted with particular caution because, for certain firms, it covers a range of countries (and products) between which experiences may differ. It is presented here merely to indicate a general tendency, and this aspect of the firm's strategy is considered more fully in the next chapter. We should note, however, that only in one case was licensing referred to as the initial form of market servicing. This presumably reflects a tendency that once licensing is chosen as the method of market servicing it is difficult to switch back to internalized production because of existing contractual obligations and the market strength which is built up by the licensee. Licensing is therefore, when compared with exporting, much more a final decision.

Table 6.4   What important factors influenced the decision to service the overseas market by overseas production?

	Examples	No. of respondents = 22	
		No. of firms mentioning	% of respondents
1	Production cost considerations	2	9
2	Transport costs	8	36
3	Access to raw materials	1	–
4	Availability of labour or other factors of production	1	–
5	Proximity to markets	11	50
6	Formal trading restrictions	9	41
7	Informal trading restrictions	10	45
8	Tax regulations	0	–
9	Government incentives in host country	1	–
10	Other (see note)	3	14

Note: Other factors mentioned were (a) freedom from exchange rate variations and the acquisition of a manufacturing base for immediately increased market share, (b) the nature of the product, (c) the acquisition of technology.

We can now consider the question of central interest – why the firms chose to invest overseas. Table 6.4 summarizes the responses to this question.

The most important single factor influencing the firm's strategy is seen as the need to be close to the market which is being supplied. This refers essentially to a need felt sometimes by the firm, and sometimes by the customer, that in order to service the market adequately close local contact is essential. This may be because it is the only effective way to adapt and modify the product to suit the local conditions, requirements or tastes, or because buyers feel safer with a local supplier. This latter consideration may arise in part because the buyer may feel that his own particular requirements can be more easily met and technical problems dealt with more readily by a local supplier, but also because he may feel safer with short supply lines – which avoid tangible dangers such as dock or transport strikes, or cater for intangible feelings that geographical distances imply greater risks in supply.

The two prominent considerations which follow this are formal and informal barriers to trading. Although separate figures are quoted in the table, if we bracket them together in the general category of formal and

informal barriers to trading then some 65 per cent of the firms saw this as a major influence on their strategy. Informal barriers in this instance take the form of nationalistic buying policies on the part of governments (and sometimes firms) or administrative and technical restrictions which weigh strongly against foreign producers supplying the market by export.

Turning to cost-based influences, the most important of these is transportation costs. This was, naturally, most important where the products were bulky (and where they had a relatively low value-added with narrow profit margins) and where costs of transport become a significant proportion of total cost. The factor which is given little emphasis in Table 6.4 is production cost considerations. This was explored in greater detail with the firms in an attempt to discover whether they had expected costs of production to be lower overseas (that is, Europe and the USA) than in the UK and whether this expectation had materialized. In addition they were asked to judge whether wage costs and productivity differed between home and overseas locations.

Only a handful of firms claimed that costs of production were significantly lower overseas, while a few claimed that costs were lower in the UK. In general, the feeling was that while productivity per man was greater overseas (with some exceptions), this was offset by higher wage costs, so that production costs were not necessarily lower. A common point which was stressed, however, was that it is extremely difficult to make a sensible comparison because the answer depends upon the scale of output which was achieved at a particular time, and because exchange rate fluctuations make it very difficult to compare costs between countries. As a result, the general feeling was that cost comparisons were only a minor part of the overseas investment decision, and one which was greatly outweighed by the other influences mentioned.

In this section we should also note that we asked the firms whether Britain's decision to join the European Economic Community had influenced their overseas production/exporting strategy (the presumption being that membership would favour exports because of the reduction in tariffs). In answering this question most of the firms claimed that the actual decision to enter the EEC had not influenced their strategy. The reason for this was that long before Britain's entry, the firms had perceived that Europe was an expanding market and had made a decision to enter that market. Although membership resulted in a reduction in tariffs, in cases where these had been an important cause of establishing overseas production, the fall in tariffs did not generally lead to a change in production strategy because it seemed most sensible to continue with the existing European subsidiary. Most of the companies were agreed, however, that if Britain were to withdraw from the EEC it would be damaging to their existing overseas business and would result,

in some cases, in a fall in exports and perhaps an increase in overseas production.

Products and markets

The answers to the questions posed in this chapter depend, to a considerable degree, upon the particular industries in which the firms operate. For instance, if production is based upon the possession of high technology processes, which may be patented, then one would expect that a licence would be easier to sell than if the product were based upon designs or processes which are readily accessible to any interested party. Similarly, to take another example, transportation costs are obviously of greater significance to a firm which produces a relatively bulky product which has a low value-added in production and which carries a low profit margin – say, some bottled drinks – than to a firm which sells high value-added, advanced electronic components. While differences between industries and products are dealt with in detail in the next chapter, we can give a general indication here of the range of products which our firms produce and sell overseas by reference to Table 6.5, which highlights some of the general characteristics of these products. We should emphasize, however, that the table conceals the fact that a particular firm may produce goods in more than one category and that its overseas investment strategy may differ between products. In addition, while a firm might be generally regarded as being in a high technology industry – say, electrical engineering – some of the products it manufactures overseas may be based upon a relatively low technology.

Table 6.5 What products does your company produce overseas?

		No. of respondents = 23	
Examples		*No. of firms mentioning*	*% of respondents*
1 New products		5	22
2 Well-established, standardized products		17	74
3 High technology products		7	30
4 Low technology products		14	61
5 High value-added products		8	35
6 Low value-added products		11	48

Nevertheless the table does give a first indication of a topic we pick up in the next chapter.

Table 6.5 indicates that a significant majority of the firms regard the products they produce overseas as being basically well-established, standardized products, often based upon a relatively low technology and with a relatively low value-added. The table does merit some further comment, however, since although the product categories themselves are quite straightforward, their inter-relationship need not be.

When considering the categories together, it would be common to assume that 'high' technology products are those which have a higher unit value-added and higher profit margins. Conversely, 'low' technology products would tend to be associated with low value-added and lower profit margins. In addition, the former would often tend to be those which are 'newer', while the latter would usually be the more well-established, standardized products. It should be recognized, however, that there may be some products which do not fit this general pattern. For instance, a firm may produce a product which is based upon a well-established, fairly low technology, and yet the product may incorporate high value-added because the firm has sufficient market power to charge a high price. The tendency would be to suppose that competition would be more fierce under these circumstances and would tend to push prices down. In general this may be true, but there are instances where the firm can retain considerable pricing power because of the managerial expertise which is necessary for efficient operations to take place: the technology and the product itself might be quite straightforward, but the co-ordination of its production and sale – 'the servicing of the market' – might require a highly efficient managerial structure. Similarly, a firm which has a new, high technology product, which is in strong demand, would be able to charge a relatively high price, which implies a high value-added in production. Whether this implies a high profit margin, however, depends upon the proportion of value-added which goes to wages and salaries. While wage differences across industries are likely in practice to be sufficiently similar that high value-added firms also have higher profit margins, in principle this need not be the case. Finally, we should distinguish, while we are discussing the subject, between profit margins and profitability, since firms which produce goods with a high value-added, but which have short production runs, are not necessarily more profitable than those whose products have a low unit value-added, but which have long production runs.

Since further discussion of this topic requires a more detailed examination of individual firms, we leave it to the next chapter. At this stage we note that while, in one or two instances, some of the qualifications alluded to above are relevant, in general our sample follows the common pattern suggested earlier. It is the standardized, lower technology, lower value-added products which are most important for overseas production (with the newer, high technology products more often exported).

The final point to consider under this heading is the general nature of the competition which the firms face. We did attempt, in this context, to identify which of the elements of competition were most important – price, quality and design, after sales-service, delivery time, and so on – but in general it proved difficult to separate these elements, since they are so inter-related and so much part of the general sales package. We confined ourselves therefore to a simple question regarding the nature of competition. Asked whether they faced many competitors, or only a few large competitors, 30 per cent of the firms suggested that their main competition was from the former category while 70 per cent suggested the latter. If anything, this tends to confirm the common view that firms which are involved in overseas production tend to be those which are in oligopolistic markets.

Licensing and exporting

In this section we consider whether export servicing of the market or licensing would have been a possibility, had the firms not established overseas production. While the export or licensing alternative to overseas production is a decision which is obviously made at an early stage in the firm's planning, we have left this to the end of our discussion since it is perhaps better appreciated when one has dealt with the other aspects of the overseas investment decision. Table 6.6 summarizes the responses to this question.

The first part of the question in Table 6.6 – whether exporting would have been a possibility if overseas production facilities had not been established – is one which has been the subject of much discussion, particularly when analysing the effects of direct investment overseas. Two opposite assumptions are usually suggested. The first is that had the UK firm not invested in overseas production, a similar investment would have been made by a non-UK firm (the so-called reverse classical assumption) so that the market, in effect, would have been lost. The alternative assumption (the so-called anti-classical assumption) is that overseas investment by the UK firm represents an addition to capacity in the overseas country which would not have taken place had the UK firm not invested – with the implication that the market could have been maintained by exporting.

In practice, of course, the real world is likely to be characterized by neither of these extremes, but in making a 'hard' assessment of the consequences of overseas investment it is convenient to take one of the extreme assumptions. Various commentators have criticized Professor

Table 6.6 If overseas production had not been established in Country X would it have been possible for you to establish or continue export sales to Country X or to license production?

		No. of respondents = 22	
Examples		*No. of firms mentioning*	*% of respondents*
1 Establish or continue export sales:			
Yes		11	50
No		11	50
2 License production overseas:			
Yes		13	60
No		8	36

Reddaway's (1968) study of the effects upon the UK economy of direct investment overseas, because of its supposed reliance upon the first of these assumptions – that export markets would have been lost (here we are concerned with the direct substitution effect between overseas production and exporting, rather than any continuing induced effect on exports resulting from overseas investment). In fact, although Reddaway did assume that a non-UK company would have undertaken a similar investment if the UK firm had not invested overseas, he recognized at various points that this does not necessarily imply a complete loss of export markets. Because the non-UK company would not be producing identical products, there would be some scope for exporting – on a much reduced scale – by the UK firm.

In an appendix to his study, Reddaway did attempt to make some estimate of the volume of exports which would have been maintained under alternative favourable, unfavourable and 'best guess' assumptions. In our case, we did not attempt the almost impossible task of ascertaining a numerical figure for the quantity of exports which would have been maintained, and contented ourselves with a yes or no choice. As Table 6.6 indicates, some 50 per cent of the firms thought that they could have exported, while the other 50 per cent thought that they would have lost the market. While at first sight this seems to suggest a position somewhere in the middle of the two extreme assumptions, in practice, of the 50 per cent of firms who thought that they could export, many felt that their exports would have been substantially lower than the sales their overseas subsidiaries had achieved: they could have held on to the market in some countries, but on a much reduced scale. The conclusion, overall, therefore, does not appear to be wildly at variance with Reddaway's qualified assumption.

With regard to the other consideration – whether the firm could have licensed production overseas – Table 6.6 indicates that 60 per cent of the firms felt that they could have licensed some of their production. In an attempt to elaborate upon this, the firms were asked what the main considerations were in the decision relating to licensing.

In some instances licensing was not a possibility because there was nothing particularly special about the product itself. The firm's production advantage lay in its management and co-ordination of supply, something which cannot be isolated from the firm and sold separately. For those firms that could conceivably have licensed, a majority view seemed to be that there was a strong desire to retain production under the firm's own control, and licensing would only really be considered as a last resort, if there were important obstacles to overseas investment or exporting. To the extent that we could identify specific reasons, the desire to retain internal control of production seemed to be based in part upon considerations of pride and identification with the product, and upon a need to maintain control over product quality and the company's general image, and in part upon the fact that licensing seemed, on the whole, to be considered less profitable than other forms of production. In addition to this, there was often a general feeling that if the firm were to maintain its competitive position in world markets it was necessary to be involved actively in those markets, because it is often only through the direct experience of producing for a market that the firm can maintain an intimate awareness of new developments and changes: learning by doing confers important dynamic benefits which help to maintain growth.

Licensing agreements were entered into, in general, where the market was not large enough to warrant overseas production and where there were obstacles (often government-inspired) to exporting, and sometimes when the product was ageing and of peripheral interest to the firm's current market thrust. Where the market was large and overseas production was warranted, the firms preferred to control this themselves. There were instances, however, where the required financial investment was considered beyond the firm's resources, or considered too risky, in part because of strong potential competition from alternative indigenous producers, who, to maintain their market position, would have forced the firm into a long and expensive competitive battle which was deemed too costly and too risky to entertain. In these instances, it was considered safer to license production.

Organization and control

In chapter 3 we emphasized that there is a qualitative difference between analysing the establishment of a new overseas subsidiary and the expansion of an already existing subsidiary. It was suggested that once the subsidiary becomes established overseas it may acquire a certain amount of independence ('a life of its own') or an identity akin to an indigenous firm overseas, and that as a consequence of this the subsidiary itself may provide a significant stimulus to further expansion overseas, or may retard contraction. In this final section we attempt to assess the importance of this factor, by presenting the answers to some questions concerning the organization of the firms and the independence of their overseas subsidiaries.

The first question that we asked our firms in this connection was about their basic structure, and about whether they were organized as an integrated international enterprise or rather as a collection of autonomous operations. The responses are summarized in Table 6.7. For many companies this was a difficult question to answer either because the situation was different for different product groups or divisions, or

Table 6.7 Are your overseas affiliates organized as essentially independent businesses or as integrated parts of an international Group operation?

	Examples	No. of respondents = 32[1]	
		No. of firms/ divisions	*% of total*
1	Are your overseas affiliates principally marketing concerns for products in the UK?	4	13
2	Do your overseas affiliates, in general, undertake manufacturing activities similar to those carried out in the UK?	21	66
3	Do your overseas affiliates mainly undertake the fabrication of finished goods from components, semi-manufactures, etc., supplied from the UK?	4	13
4	Do your overseas affiliates provide individual facilities/services not available elsewhere in the Group?	3	9

Note: 1 Respondents included divisions of firms.

because some affiliates might fulfil both production and marketing roles. We have attempted to take such considerations into account by classifying such companies under more than one heading. Hence the number of responses (32) is more than the number of firms (23) in the sample.

In only a handful of cases do affiliates provide individual facilities or services not available elsewhere in the Group. These instances arose, moreover, through mergers or acquisitions of foreign subsidiaries which had access to particular expertise. Typically economies of scale were large and there was thus no way in which the technology or special expertise could be transferred economically to other sites. Similarly, there were only a few instances where overseas affiliates undertook the fabrication of finished goods from materials, etc. supplied from the United Kingdom. This form of organization tended to occur in two particular situations. First, in the pharmaceutical industry where regulations in many countries circumscribe the import of finished drugs; the firms concerned thus undertake the final fabrication of the finished drugs locally after importing most of the ingredients from the United Kingdom. Second, in defence contracting where a local supplier is often deemed essential by government purchasing agencies. Often, however, the local facilities required in these cases need to be little more than assembly or maintenance workshops for equipment imported in parts from the United Kingdom.

The relative paucity of overseas affiliates cited as being principally marketing concerns for products produced in the UK probably reflects our concentration in this study on large, well-established companies. We were frequently told that the initial foray into direct investment overseas was to establish a marketing or distribution concern. This would typically be superseded by some form of limited manufacturing capacity. Only when the viability of local manufacture had been established would full-scale production facilities be built.

In general, the majority of the firms in our sample were organized as a collection of essentially similar entities whose locations were determined by the considerations set out in Table 6.4. These individual manufacturing units tended, on the whole, to source their raw materials, components, etc. from local suppliers. It is evident from Table 6.7 that only four firms or divisions reported a significant amount of intra-company trade in input items.

Given the general pattern that the affiliates of most of our firms carry out activities similar to those undertaken in the United Kingdom, we considered the degree to which central direction or guidance was provided by the parent. In order to do this, we asked our sample companies a series of questions about the degree of autonomy accorded to their overseas affiliates with respect to (a) pricing or marketing decisions, (b) the organization of R & D activities, and (c) investment

Table 6.8 Are your overseas subsidiaries and branches allowed a large degree of autonomy? To what extent are their pricing, marketing, etc. decisions subject to approval by central management?

	Examples	*No. of respondents = 23*	
		No. of times mentioned	*% of respondents*
1	Decisions made by central management	3	13
2	Decisions made by local management but subject to approval by central management	7	30
3	Decisions made by local management but budgets subject to periodic central review	4	17
4	Decisions left largely to local management	9	39

decisions. The answers are summarized in Tables 6.8, 6.9 and 6.10. By its nature, the classification in Table 6.8 is largely fairly arbitrary. At one extreme, it would be impractical for central management to vet every transaction made throughout the world. At the other extreme, it is unlikely that local autonomy would survive a consistent run of losses. Our general impression, however, is that overseas affiliates are allowed a large degree of autonomy as regards pricing and marketing decisions as long as they produce satisfactory performance. Apart from a few instances where multiple sourcing, and hence potential conflicts of interest arise, central management limits its role in pricing and marketing to one of trouble-shooting and general monitoring of performance.

We now consider the situation as regards the organization of research and development activities. It seems reasonable to suggest that, *ceteris paribus*, the more centralized the R & D capability of a company, the greater is the potential for central control and direction. Table 6.9 categorizes the companies as fitting one of three broad descriptions.

Care needs to be taken over the interpretation of the figures in Table 6.9, as many factors can influence the spread of R & D facilities. For example, of the cases where the R & D capability is reported as being spread across affiliates, three correspond to the instances highlighted in Table 6.7 where special expertise has been gained by way of merger or acquisition. In two further cases, it was the particular historical development of the companies in question which determined the

Table 6.9 How does your company organize its R & D activities? Is product or process research and development centrally located or spread across affiliates?

		No. of respondents = 23	
Examples		*Frequency of cases*	*% of respondents*
1 Central Research and Development facility		6	26
2 Central Research facility with some development capability in affiliates		9	39
3 Research and Development capability spread across affiliates		8	35

location of R & D facilities, rather than a conscious decision to spread the capability across the affiliates. In 65 per cent of the companies, however, a central research facility exists although in some cases development work is also carried out in individual affiliates. Such findings indicate a degree of potential control which refutes any suggestion of completely autonomous overseas affiliates.

We now turn to the final two questions in this section which are related to investment by overseas affiliates. We asked our sample of firms whether it is the parent or the affiliate that perceives investment opportunities, and how far approval for investment projects is required from central management. The answers are summarized in Table 6.10. Clearly, overseas affiliates are encouraged to initiate investment proposals. The large majority (more than 80 per cent) of respondents admitted a positive role for local management in identifying possible opportunities. But in most cases the parent company either had a standard set of investment criteria which had to be fulfilled, or all capital expenditure above a certain level had to be approved by central management. In only eight companies – of which five were cited above as having R & D capability across affiliates – was authority devolved sufficiently that affiliates could undertake capital expenditure up to a certain limit on their own volition. Even in these companies major acquisitions and investments, and questions of overall corporate development, were the province of central management.

In summary, therefore, it appears that we may divide the companies in our sample broadly as having one of two types of organization. On the one hand, there are companies (conglomerates would perhaps be a

Table 6.10 What control does the parent company exercise over its overseas affiliates with regard to further investment by the affiliates?

(a) In general, who perceives the investment opportunity?

No. of respondents = 22

		Frequency of cases	*% of respondents*
1	The parent company	4	18
2	The overseas affiliate	12	55
3	Either	6	27

(b) How far is approval required from the parent company?

No. of respondents = 23

		Frequency of cases	*% of respondents*
1	There is a standard 'book of rules' for all investment decisions	15	65
2	Standard rules apply only to capital expenditure above a certain level	8	35

more apt term) where the individual units either provide specialized services or are significant in some other way, for example in size. In such cases, the role of Head Office is limited. On the other hand, the majority of the companies in the sample have overseas affiliates whose autonomy is largely restricted to day-to-day trading operations. In general, while overseas subsidiaries provide a positive impetus to overseas expansion by identifying new opportunities, parent company control is exerted through the monitoring of performance and the control of capital expenditure, and by the fact that affiliates are dependent on central research facilities.

III Concluding comments

By considering stage by stage the various decisions which must be made (sometimes implicitly) in the formation of an overseas investment strategy, we hope we have given a first indication of the factors which the firms in our sample consider of most significance. In their view, the main advantages that they possessed which enabled them to compete overseas, either by exports or by overseas production, lay in the quality or design of their products or in their special management expertise. They were attracted to overseas markets by the size and rate of growth of these markets, rather than by stagnation in the UK market. Before overseas production was undertaken a majority of our firms were supplying overseas markets by exporting, but formal and informal trading restrictions were among the main reasons why they decided to establish production overseas. Other factors were the advantages of proximity to overseas markets and transport cost advantages. Relative production costs at home and overseas did not seem to be important for our particular firms.

The products produced overseas were, in general, well established and standardized, embodying low technology and with low value-added. Some products were high technology, but in a number of cases firms with high technology products preferred to manufacture these in the UK and export them, partly on account of the low overall level of demand for the products concerned and partly because of the specialized expertise needed to produce them. In general, whatever the type of product they exported or made overseas, our firms faced a small number of large competitors rather than many competitors.

Somewhat surprisingly, 50 per cent of our firms thought that they could have gone on exporting if they had not decided to produce overseas, but this does not mean that they could have achieved the increase in sales which production overseas usually brought about. Similarly, a high proportion of our firms (60 per cent) thought they could have licensed some of their products or processes to other firms overseas if they had not produced there themselves. Here again, however, they thought that there were advantages in establishing production overseas. They were able to keep control over quality, and in addition they believed that licensing would have been less profitable, and less beneficial to the long-term growth of the firm, than producing themselves. They tended to license only where the market was not large enough to warrant overseas production or where there were obstacles to exporting or setting up local production. The existence of strong overseas competitors was another reason why licensing had been undertaken.

Finally, it appears that in some instances, because of their long life, the overseas subsidiaries of our sample firms have acquired a certain amount of autonomy, and hence provide a positive impetus to overseas expansion. This independence is limited, however, by central control of capital and research and development expenditure, and by the monitoring of performance.

The questionnaire answers considered in this chapter have provided a useful background for our study, but they nevertheless suggest that a more detailed investigation of individual firms is required. We turn therefore in the next chapter to more detailed case studies of the firms in our sample. This enables us both to elaborate upon the factors discussed in this section, and to qualify and draw together the somewhat general evidence which this chapter has provided.

CHAPTER SEVEN

Why do firms manufacture overseas?
Evidence from the case studies

In this chapter we present our case studies of individual firms. The first thing we require in considering these firms is some method of classifying them into manageable and consistent categories, as opposed to merely examining each firm in isolation. There are various classifications which could be adopted: we could classify the firms according to the broad motive for investing overseas, according to whether exporting was a possibility or not, according to the destination of the investment, and so on. From the various alternatives, we have chosen to categorize firms according to their industrial grouping. With this, we can highlight any parallels among the firms as to motivation, possibilities for exporting, etc. and, at the same time, distinguish clearly any important differences which exist between industries.

I The industries

The broad industrial groupings consist of food, drink and tobacco; mechanical and instrument engineering (including motor vehicle components); electrical engineering; chemicals (including pharmaceuticals); textiles; paper and publishing; and, finally, metal goods and other manufactures. Within each of these industrial classifications we have adopted a flexible manner of presentation – sometimes dealing with a firm individually and sometimes grouping the firms together. The flexibility seemed to be the most appropriate way of allowing comparisons and distinctions to be made, while at the same time avoiding the tedium which can easily arise from following an unduly rigid presentational framework. At the end of each section, the evidence from a particular firm or group of firms is summarized very briefly, in order to facilitate comparisons with the material of the previous chapter. In those few instances where firms have expressed a desire to remain anonymous, we include only very brief details of any general tendencies which the anonymous companies exhibit.

II   Food, drink and tobacco

This first industrial grouping provides the largest source of direct investment overseas. Within this, we consider the cases of three firms: United Biscuits, who produce biscuits and snacks; Cadbury-Schweppes, who produce confectionery and soft drinks; and Rothmans International, who produce cigarettes.

United Biscuits

United Biscuits was formed as the result of a merger in 1948 between McVities and Macfarlane, and the later addition of Crawfords in 1962, and Macdonalds in 1965. The firm has traditionally been a manufacturer of products which have a low unit value-added, which are produced in large volume and which rely quite heavily upon advertising in order to sustain market shares. Most biscuit and snacks products are relatively straightforward to manufacture (and copy) and brand loyalty is an important aspect of competition. In most geographical markets, United Biscuits' competitors are the large US firms and smaller local manufacturers, although in Europe there are large manufacturers in France and Germany.

United Biscuits has traditionally relied upon the UK market for its sales, but in the early 1960s, as the Group expanded, some rationalization was necessary, since the constituent parts of the Group had previously been allowed to carry on as largely separate entities. Having reorganized its domestic operations, the firm sought to expand into overseas markets. This was considered desirable since potential growth in the UK was limited as United Biscuits already possessed about 40 per cent of the biscuit market and 20–30 per cent of the snack market.

The firm's major expansion into overseas production in Europe came in 1970 when it purchased a crisp manufacturer with production units in Holland and Belgium. The Benelux countries offered a good location from which to service this market. Subsequent rationalization led to manufacturing being concentrated at one major site in Belgium – providing for sales in France, Germany, Belgium and Holland. Other European production is located in Spain, where the firm produces soft buns and cakes, but it also has marketing operations in France and Denmark.

Europe accounts for only some 10 per cent of United Biscuits' overseas investment and the other 90 per cent is located in the United States. The initial expansion occurred in 1974 when the firm acquired Keebler, the second largest US biscuit firm after Nabisco. United Biscuits prefers to expand via acquisition, because this provides the immediate benefits of product markets and distribution networks which have already been proved. Entry into the market via the establishment of a greenfield operation usually implies a relatively small scale of operations to begin with and so makes it easier for major competitors to retaliate. Given this preference, an important reason for expanding in the United States was the non-availability of suitable firms to acquire in Europe. Thus, although United Biscuits had originally intended to expand principally into Europe, the firm turned to the United States when a suitable opportunity arose.

The upshot of these developments is that 35 per cent of the Group's production is located in the USA and 5 per cent in continental Europe. The remaining 60 per cent of production is located in the UK with almost all of this being sold domestically.

There are several difficulties which the firm faces in attempting to service overseas markets by exporting. First, transport costs become a significant element of costs because the products are relatively bulky. In addition, because of the large volumes involved, transportation tends to be by sea. In nearby markets this may not impose too great a problem, but where the distances are great (for instance, Australia or the USA) the delay reduces the time available to sell the product within its optimum 'shelf-life'. Although the products may be supported by advertising, particularly in the early stages of market penetration, competition from local products may be strong, and the transport premium is a significant handicap. Second, while there may be various problems with exporting which are specific to a particular country – for instance, formal trading restrictions in Spain or differences between the UK and Germany in permitted additives – the other main general difficulty in exporting concerns the desirability of being close to the market. Local knowledge and experience is regarded as essential if the firm is to assess the particular combination of product specification, advertising, etc., which are required if a significant market share is to be achieved.

As a result of these and other difficulties, exporting, for United Biscuits, has been only a small activity which has never constituted more than 3 to 4 per cent of domestic production.

Cadbury-Schweppes

Cadbury-Schweppes presents an interesting case which has many similarities with United Biscuits. On the confectionery (Cadbury) side of the business, the overseas marketing philosophy was, until the 1960s, to service by exports, markets in the countries of the Commonwealth and the United States, where tastes in chocolate are not dissimilar to those of the UK consumers. Since then the company has moved into other markets, particularly continental Europe.

Cadbury has, with few exceptions, based its production in the UK and Ireland. The basic reason for this is that there are significant economies of scale in chocolate manufacture and hence it is natural to base production in the British and Irish markets where the company has very large market shares. Licences are not in general given out by Cadbury, principally because quality control of the product is very difficult to maintain.

In the case of the European market, exporting is again the most obvious form of market servicing, in particular because of limited demand which makes overseas production uneconomic to establish. The preference in continental Europe is for a relatively smooth and liquid chocolate, and British-style chocolate serves only a 'fringe' demand. In contrast with their strategy in the English-speaking markets, where the products are heavily supported by advertising (and with the exception of France, where heavy advertising has led to a strong demand for chocolate-covered biscuits), Cadbury does not advertise to any great extent in continental Europe. Apart from the basic difference in tastes (which implies that advertising would be unlikely to succeed) there are considerable differences in legislation between countries, which makes it difficult to establish a common advertising strategy. In general Cadbury's experience fits the pattern of other European firms. There are no 'European companies' as such: most firms produce chocolate for their domestic markets and then export the limited amount that they can.

For the soft drinks (Schweppes) side of the business overseas production is the more normal practice, often based upon a licence or franchise arrangement. Exporting relatively low priced soft drinks from the United Kingdom is not really a viable strategy, simply because the sheer bulk of liquid means that transport costs are high in relation to the product price: depending upon local conditions, Schweppes' objective is to have their manufacturers serve a radius of about 100 km.

The Schweppes products have a reputation of being quality drinks and sales are dependent upon maintaining this image. Granted that overseas production is desirable because of transport costs, the company originally did not license production for fear of losing quality control. After some experience, however, they found that this difficulty could be overcome (by taking water samples from the manufacturers, by buying the product in local shops, etc.) and the company now has a preference for licensing production overseas, so long as they are satisfied that the franchisee can maintain market growth. The company aims for market growth, and licensing is the easiest and quickest way of obtaining this, since it is the franchisee who provides most of the finance and manages the operation. Schweppes provide the franchisee with the use of the trade mark, the 'secret' essences which give the drink its taste, and comprehensive advice in formulating a business plan for distribution, finance and machinery. Schweppes then handle the extensive advertising required to promote the drink. In general, the company is content to follow this form of manufacture so long as the franchisee meets their objective of market growth. Where this is not maintained, or where no suitable franchisee can be found, Schweppes set up production under their own control.

Internationally, Schweppes is now the third largest purveyor of soft drinks, after the two Cola companies. Their philosophy is to franchise in any stable (developed or developing) country where the market is likely to be sufficiently large to ensure the economies of scale and quality control which efficient production requires.

Rothmans International

Rothmans International is an international group of companies primarily engaged in the manufacture, distribution and sale of high-quality, premium priced tobacco products in markets throughout the world. The Group was formed in 1972 following the merger of Martin Brinkmann of West Germany, Tabacofina of Belgium, Turmac of Holland with companies and other interests owned by Rothmans Tobacco (Holdings) Limited, using the UK publicly quoted company Carreras Limited as the vehicle for amalgamation. In 1978, the Group was further strengthened by the addition of a majority stake in Rothmans of Pall Mall Canada Limited. The original merger brought into the Group the Dunhill Group of companies, at the time a majority owned subsidiary of Carreras Limited. With the acquisition of the Canadian interests in 1978, the Group's non-tobacco interests were extended to include Carling O'Keefe.

In a league of leading international cigarette companies in the free world, the Group occupies fourth position, behind BAT, Philip Morris and R. J. Reynolds, but ahead of American Brands and Imperial Group. In terms of turnover it also ranks 24th in the *Times* Top 1000 and holds 220th position in the *Fortune* 500 largest industrial companies outside the USA. Approximately 33,000 people are employed by the Group worldwide, about 60 per cent of whom are in Europe.

Operations are usually conducted through a large number of wholly and partially owned subsidiaries and associates, including a significant number of publicly quoted companies. The Group manufactures tobacco products either directly or in partnership with local interests under licence or sub-contract arrangements in more than 50 factories in 33 countries, approximately half of which are located in the EEC.

Although the products themselves are broadly similar in appearance, their production involves the use of sophisticated high technology equipment. The production process is highly automated and there are substantial economies of scale in production – modern machines can make and pack between 6000 and 7000 cigarettes per minute. Advertising is an important method of securing market share for any brand.

The production strategy of a company such as Rothmans is influenced by the economies of scale already referred to, but is determined even more by government intervention in the form of tariff barriers, local employment considerations, etc. As a general rule, EEC production centres service their own domestic markets – the exceptions being France and Italy where the existence of government monopolies restricts the freedom of companies to manufacture. The production source for exports to other parts of the world is dependent upon marketing considerations (e.g. 'Made in the United Kingdom' is an important factor in many countries) and upon available manufacturing capacity. The latter also comes into play if, for example, a temporary increase in demand means that traditional sources of supply can no longer cope. In such an instance the volume peak could be satisfied with another factory with spare capacity, possibly even located in another country.

However, switching production between countries to satisfy more permanent changes in demand or to achieve rationalization measures is not part of the Group's strategy. This is partly due to the existence of the large, partly owned, publicly quoted subsidiaries and associates referred to earlier but also to the Group's overall operating principles. Rothmans works in partnership with local governments and interests in the countries in which it operates. It is the responsibility of each local operation to take steps to redress any imbalance between production capacity and demand, making use of Group resources to achieve an optimum solution, e.g. it may prove advantageous to make use of surplus manufacturing capacity in a neighbouring country rather than embark upon a major capital expenditure programme.

In deciding whether or not local production capacity or licence arrangements should be established in new markets, the availability of spare capacity in established markets is often of little importance. Equally, because of the low weight, compact nature of the Group's products, transportation costs play only a minor role. Transport costs are not insignificant, however, particularly because of the relatively high cost of insuring the loads. Of far greater importance are import and other tariff barriers and, in developing countries, the desire of governments to create an industrial base and limit hard currency outflows. In some cases Rothmans is obliged to take a minority shareholding in a government-owned company, and then license production.

Food, drink and tobacco: summary

United Biscuits
Overseas markets mainly serviced by overseas production.

1 *Principal reasons for overseas production*
   Desire to expand/large domestic market share. Transport costs. Advantages of proximity to markets.

2 *Method*
Acquisition.

3 *Location*
Europe and USA.

4 *Type of product*
Relatively low technology. Low value-added. Large volumes. Brand loyalty/advertising.

Cadbury-Schweppes
Overseas markets for confectionery mainly serviced by exports because of limited overseas demand plus large economies of scale in production. Overseas markets for soft drinks mainly serviced by overseas production.

1 *Principal reasons for overseas production* (soft drinks)
Desire to expand. Transport costs.

2 *Method*
Franchising (control of overseas investment when no suitable franchise).

3 *Location*
Worldwide.

4 *Type of product*
Low technology. Low value-added. Large volumes. Brand loyalty advertising.

Rothmans International
Overseas market mainly serviced by overseas production, but with some exporting.

1 *Principal reasons for overseas production*
Desire for expansion. Historical pattern of original constituent companies. Trade restrictions. Transport/insurance costs.

2 *Method*
Greenfield investment and licensing.

3 *Location*
Europe and worldwide.

4 *Type of product*
High technology process, low technology product. High value-added. Large volumes. Economies of scale. Brand loyalty.

III Electrical engineering

The electrical engineering industry is usually taken to be one which falls into the category of high technology. In many instances this label is well applied (particularly in defence-related industries) but it conceals the fact that many firms in the electrical engineering industry also produce very well established and standardized products (often in conjunction with high technology goods). The firms we consider in this industry represent a variety of different experiences and show the diversity which is contained in any broad industrial classification. We consider the cases of Thorn EMI (concentrating principally upon Thorn EMI Lighting), Racal, Ferranti, and two anonymous electrical engineering companies. Since there is this diversity, it is helpful if we relate their stories rather more in terms of the split between high and relatively low technology products than between the firms as such.

Within electrical engineering, the part of the industry which is based upon the most highly sophisticated products is contained within the defence area. All but one of our firms have some direct presence in defence-related industry, with the most prominent (in terms of percentage of its sales) being Ferranti.

The products in the defence area are sold in relatively small volume and are based upon intensive research and development (usually protected by patents). The aim is to provide the customer with the best available weapon or system. Given the nature of the purchasers (government agencies) and the fact that the appeal of the products is their advanced technology, competition is not usually in price, and is based upon the ability to deliver an advanced and reliable system.

There is strong competition in technology from a number of firms in Western Europe and the USA, where education and research are sophisticated enough to support advanced technology. Most countries have a strong preference to buy from domestic producers, so that competition is particularly strong where they produce similar systems. Any overseas sales which are gained, however, are likely to be extremely profitable, since the heavy research and development costs of the product are likely to have been covered by domestic sales. Without exception, for our firms, the production centres for defence equipment are based in the UK and (sometimes) in the USA. The case of *Ferranti* is sufficient to illustrate the important aspects of this part of the industry.

Because of the strong 'buy local' policy of most countries (which restricts the range of products that can be sold in a particular market) and because the demand for any particular product is relatively limited by its nature, Ferranti considers it uneconomic to establish production centres overseas. If any contracts are won, these are supplied by exporting from the UK. The general strategy when selling overseas is to work through local agents (sometimes a similar company which is not in competition with that product) or as a sub-contractor to a local prime contractor, in an attempt to circumvent the preferential buying policies of foreign governments. The agent network attempts to overcome the political problem in selling and also to provide a local presence. Hence, despite the fact that Ferranti might appear to have very little formal investment in a particular country it may, together with its agent, have a large presence, providing not only goods, but also after-sales service, training, etc.

The situation in the United States is less restrictive in that US agencies are less worried about who owns the company, so long as the factory is based in America and staffed by Americans. For this reason, and the fact that the American market is larger (and hence more able to sustain an economic production unit) Ferranti manufacture in the United States: unless the product is produced there it is highly unlikely that it will be bought.

As regards licensing, Ferranti does take in and give out some licenses, usually where this is necessary to fill a gap in the company's technology. Taking out a licence, however, is usually only considered as a last resort, and it can be viewed within the company as a technical defeat.

The remainder of our firms in the electrical engineering industry produce a range of goods, from advanced electronic systems to standardized lighting equipment. In general, it appears that when products are relatively sophisticated, embodying a high value-added, such cost-based influences as transport costs and relative production costs are fairly unimportant in the location decision. In these instances, firms appear content to base production in the UK and then export to overseas markets. Where overseas production does take place, this is generally due to trading restrictions (including preferential buying policies). In the case of more standardized products (usually with much lower profit margins) cost considerations are much more important – though even then, trading restrictions and resistance from buyers to foreign products are significant. Finally, in considering the remainder of the firms, it also becomes apparent that the importance of historical accident cannot be ignored.

Discounting Ferranti, with its heavy emphasis on defence work, the two of our firms which most clearly fit the description of high technology companies are *Racal* and one of the anonymous companies. Competition for these companies comes from firms in the USA and Europe. All of the firms have strong incentive to gain overseas sales in order to spread the heavy research and development costs which are associated with their products. Although the competition is often based upon design and technology, price can become an important factor where these are common between competitors. Because the products are not usually sold to the general public, advertising is of a more specialized trade nature, though still designed to gain market shares. The products are usually designed around a 'core' of universal application which is then adapted for particular overseas markets.

It appears that, almost without exception, where the products are based upon a high technology, the value-added in production (and profitability) is sufficiently high for transport costs and relative production costs to be

109

given little weight in the location decision. The firms seem more than happy to base production in the UK and then supply overseas markets by exporting. Where overseas production does occur this appears to be due to strong 'buy local' policies of overseas purchasers, or to historical circumstances rather than dissatisfaction with the UK as a production base. We can take some brief examples to illustrate this pattern.

Both Racal and the anonymous company manufacture electronic systems and radar in the UK and export them all over the world. In both cases, these parts of the firm originated and grew in the UK and there is little reason to shift production overseas. The products are highly profitable, but have a relatively limited demand in any one market, and it is therefore most efficient to concentrate production in the home base and supply overseas markets by exporting. Overseas investments, when they occur in this part of the business, take the form of marketing subsidiaries through which exports are sold.

Although we cannot go into any details about the anonymous company we have mentioned, it appears that its most usually exported products are from the high technology end of the electrical engineering spectrum. Where overseas production occurs this has been due to the 'buy local' policies of government and similar agencies: in order to win the market it has been necessary to produce overseas. Those overseas investments which the company did undertake, which seem to be direct substitution of foreign for UK production, occurred in the lower technology range of their business.

We will consider the lower technology parts of the electrical engineering industry when we deal with the remaining companies in the sample, but before leaving the higher technology end of the spectrum we briefly consider the overseas operations of Racal (which exhibits some trends similar to the anonymous company).

Racal consists of five main divisions – the original radio communications division, the data communications division, and those acquired from Decca which are now known as Marine Electronics, Defence Radar and Avionics, and Energy Resources. Most of the production of the radio communications division has been, and is, carried out in the UK. Markets in Europe, Africa and the Middle East are serviced by exports from the UK. There is some production in the USA, South Africa and Australia, to service their respective markets, essentially because of local government pressure to have an indigenous production base. Where this pressure has not been present, however, markets have been serviced by exports from the UK.

Similarly, the old Decca businesses manufactured traditionally in the UK and then exported, and Racal have maintained this pattern. With the remaining division however – Data Communications – production is largely based in the USA. The essential reason for this is that Racal originally acted as the European distribution agent for a US company which supplied modems (which take signals from computers, or other digital sources, and modulate them so that they can be transmitted along telephone lines). Racal subsequently took over the US company and naturally retained the existing production centre. Production and research is carried out in the USA, although there is an increasing amount in the UK.

The remaining firms we consider in this industry are Thorn EMI Lighting (part of Thorn EMI) and the remaining anonymous company. These companies (though not of course Thorn EMI as a whole) are taken as representing the lower technology range of the electrical engineering industry.

Again, we cannot go into any details about our remaining anonymous company, but we can point to a general trend. This company manufactures products which are essentially standardized, using a relatively low technology. The markets for the products are quite mature and competition is strong. Tariffs on the products are often significant (particularly in developing countries which have attempted to encourage indigenous manufacturing) and transport costs are significant in relation to value and weight. As a result, exporting is quite limited and most overseas markets are serviced by overseas production (which is long-standing for the company). There is some exporting, but this is usually for small amounts of non-standard, speciality production.

Our remaining firm, Thorn EMI, produces a range of both high technology and standardized goods. As a general observation, Thorn EMI claim that they can usually service overseas markets for higher technology goods by exporting from the UK. With lower technology goods, however, they find that exporting is very difficult, mainly on account of transport costs, and that overseas production is often required. For present purposes, we can concentrate on the more standardized products, by considering the case of Thorn EMI Lighting.

The Thorn company was started over fifty years ago, by Jules Thorn, as a manufacturer of light sources. Thorn is now the major company in the UK in the manufacture of both light sources and lighting equipment, and is also a market leader in the Old Commonwealth countries. In Europe, Thorn's major competitors are Osram and Philips, although there are smaller competitors in most countries, particularly in more specialized lighting markets. Generally speaking, competition is strong for standard lighting equipment and sources, and is mainly in price, but for non-standard products quality and design are of greater importance.

There is a strong incentive to gain overseas sales because in such standardized product areas (with narrow profit margins) volume production is essential. Advertising expenditure is relatively low (between 1 and 4 per cent of sales) in part because many of the products are not aimed at the consumer market: advertising as such tends to be in trade journals. Thorn feel that any competitive advantages which they have are based essentially upon management expertise, the quality and design of their products, and a technology which is at least as good as, and often better than, that of their competitors.

Until the 1960s, Thorn's strategy in overseas markets was to manufacture in the UK and to sell through overseas agents. They then decided to buy out these agents, in order to gain greater control of the marketing effort, but continued to use the UK manufacturing base to supply overseas markets. This exporting strategy was generally successful. Since the mid-1970s, however, Thorn feel that the strategy has been increasingly unsuccessful because Britain's competitive position as a low-cost producer has been eroded by high inflation coupled with an uncompetitive exchange rate. Whereas in the mid-1970s Thorn were more efficient than both Osram and Philips (the two main continental competitors) they are now less efficient: they still have a technical advantage but in commercial terms they have dropped behind.

Taking Europe as the example, the main difficulties in servicing overseas markets with exports from the UK are the extra costs of transport and the greater distance from the market. As Thorn's other (usually cost) advantages have been eroded, these difficulties have assumed a greater and greater significance. This is illustrated by the development of Thorn's European operations.

In the early 1960s Thorn established a factory to produce light sources and light fittings in Italy. Despite this move, exporting from the UK remained the principal method of servicing European markets. Over the last six or seven years, however, Thorn argue that the high sterling exchange rate, and the presence of high domestic inflation, has meant that the Italian operations have become much more efficient as a source of supply for Europe. For instance, distribution costs for UK exports might typically be about 12 per cent of total costs, whereas distribution costs for the same market supplied from Italy are only about 6 per cent. In a market where price competition is significant, this is obviously a retarding factor for UK exports. The result has been that Thorn have now switched much of their former production, for export to Europe, from the UK to Italy. At the same time, Thorn have established factories in Sweden and Germany to manufacture light fittings (for essentially the same reasons). Light sources for these markets are imported from either the UK or (increasingly) Italy.

In concluding our discussion of the electrical engineering industry, we can briefly consider the attitude of the firms to licensing. We have already indicated that, in the case of Ferranti, there is a great reluctance to take in a licence, and they suggest that this is often true of similar companies. The company are willing to do so, however, as a last resort, if they have an important deficiency in the area of technology in question. This viewpoint is not dissimilar to that expressed by Racal and the anonymous higher technology company.

In the case of Racal's production of modems, they have granted licences only where they have been obliged to do so in order to service the local market. For instance, they license production in one particular country because although the Post Office wanted the product they insisted on production by a local manufacturer. In Europe, Racal licensed a firm in West Germany in the hope that this firm would win a contract with the *Bundespost* (which also required local production). The contract did not materialize, however, and Racal withdrew the licence.

The first anonymous company also suggests that the taking in of a licence is a last resort, which occurs when it needs to supplement its own technology. Although it did take in quite a number of licences from US firms in the 1960s, these are now not so readily available, as the US firms now prefer to establish their own manufacturing facilities in Europe. For its own part, the anonymous company is willing to license out the manufacture of 'old' products, but prefers to produce the 'new' ones itself, since this is generally more profitable and helps to maintain the company's technological advantage.

Finally, the remaining anonymous company is involved in only a small number of licensing arrangements. Where the market is considered potentially large it invests in production itself. Where the market is not considered large enough to warrant capital expenditure by itself, however, it will license to other firms.

Electrical engineering: summary

High technology products
Overseas markets serviced mainly by exports, with some significant overseas production.

1 *Principal reasons for overseas production*
   Nationalism and trade restrictions. Historical accident.

2 *Method*
   Acquisition and greenfield investment.

3 *Location*
   Europe, USA and Old Commonwealth.

4 *Type of product*
   High value-added. Low volumes. Research and development intensive.

Low technology products
Overseas markets mainly serviced by overseas production.

1 *Principal reasons for overseas production*
   Transport costs. Relative production costs. Nationalism/trade restrictions.

2 *Method*
   Overseas investment (acquisition and greenfield). Some licensing.

3 *Location*
   Europe, USA and Commonwealth.

4 *Type of product*
   Low/medium value-added. Large volumes. Based on know-how.

IV   Chemicals (including pharmaceuticals)

We consider four companies in this group, two of them pharmaceutical, one chemical, and one chemical subsidiary of a mining and manufacturing group. The pharmaceutical companies are The Wellcome Foundation and Glaxo. The chemical companies are British Petroleum and an anonymous company. It will be convenient to consider the pharmaceutical companies together.

Pharmaceuticals

Both Glaxo and Wellcome are companies which pioneer new drugs and then produce and market them. Research and development is therefore a vital activity. Because of the high level of scientific and technical staff needed, and also because of the importance of good facilities, research is concentrated in a small number of locations. In the case of Wellcome there are two R & D centres, one in the UK and one in the USA. The company feels that it is important to do R & D in the USA – they have been doing it there for seventy-five years – because of the access it gives them to the best technology. Moreover, with two research centres, Wellcome are able to hedge their bets. There is close contact, which is increasing, between the centres. In Glaxo's case research and development is mostly done in the UK. Development work however is done in many places around the world.

Production of pharmaceuticals is divided into two principal activities (a) primary production (the manufacture of the raw material/active ingredients) and (b) secondary production (the fabrication of pills, creams, etc., plus packaging). In Glaxo's case almost all primary production has been in the UK. There is some primary production in India (because of government restrictions on imports) and in Australia (with an investment which started as a milk plant in the 1920s and which was subsequently used for the fermentation of penicillin). These cases

114

apart, however, investment in manufacturing overseas has been in secondary production. Investment in primary production tends to be concentrated because it has relatively high investment costs compared with secondary production – for example the production of Betnovate involves a number of complicated chemical stages involving a large fermentation process, which finally reduces to a small quantity of the active ingredient. Glaxo are however now investing in primary production in Singapore for the manufacture of an anti-ulcer drug, Zantac. Singapore is well placed in terms of duty considerations and access to markets. In addition it has a good scientific infrastructure, which is very important for such a skilled base operation. Singapore is Glaxo's first large venture into primary production outside the UK. There was small primary production in Italy, but this was a special case, relating to the absence of patent protection for drugs in Italy. It was later disposed of and there is now only secondary production in Italy.

A consideration concerning primary production is that in the past one primary factory could supply a large part of the world. In the case of Glaxo however they have experienced a ten-fold growth in sales over the last fifteen years and this means they have needed more primary plant. The question was whether they should build a larger factory in the UK or have two factories in different locations. The decision was taken to separate primary production partly because of the reduction in the risk of stoppages, etc. that this entailed.

Wellcome now have secondary operations in forty countries and have marketing operations in many others. However, they have only four plants where they manufacture active ingredients.

Pharmaceutical companies such as Wellcome and Glaxo prefer to export from the UK, and they establish overseas manufacturing facilities only where the market is large enough to justify economic secondary production or where other advantages accrue. In most European countries, for example, it is impossible to import finished drugs from the UK because of non-tariff barriers. For instance, in Italy local secondary manufacture is obligatory before products can be sold on the human medical market, and the position is the same for certain products in France, Belgium and Spain. Wellcome had particular difficulties in establishing itself in France, but finally did so in 1965 by buying up a pharmaceutical company in Monaco, which has access to France. In Germany there is no obligation for secondary manufacture to take place before products can be sold on the human medical market, but there is an exception (as in many other countries) in the case of foot and mouth disease vaccine, and Wellcome therefore manufactures it locally. Other drugs are exported to Germany from the UK, although there are extensive marketing facilities in Germany and in countries not requiring secondary manufacture, for example Holland, Portugal and the Scandinavian countries.

115

Overseas subsidiaries tend to supply their home markets only, although there may be some export trade if surplus capacity is available. There appears to be little switching of production in response to exchange rates, inflation rates, etc., because of the administrative problems involved in conforming to all the regulations to which the pharmaceutical industry is subject.

When pharmaceutical companies establish manufacturing facilities overseas, they sometimes set up a greenfield operation and sometimes acquire existing firms. They usually have to provide new facilities especially designed for the drugs to be manufactured. Strict quality and safety control is essential – for example Glaxo cannot use the same factory to produce penicillin and other drugs and then expect to be able to export to the USA. US laws do not allow mixed production because of the possibility of cross-contamination in the production process. In the UK, on the other hand, there are no such regulations, although care is of course taken to make sure that there is no danger of cross-contamination.

The pattern in the drug industry appears to be a consistent one. Research and development takes place in a very small number of centres. The manufacture of active ingredients also takes place in a small number of locations. When there are no limitations on exporting, the drug companies prefer to export finished drugs from established centres such as the UK and simply rely on marketing operations in the receiving countries. Where, however, it is obligatory to undertake secondary manufacture in the country where drugs are to be sold, the pharmaceutical companies establish secondary manufacture. The extent of this secondary manufacture is to some extent dependent on history. Glaxo, for example, had its main geographical areas of interest in the Old Commonwealth and areas with British ties. Over the years however they have steadily moved into Europe, Japan and South America. They now have subsidiaries in almost all countries of Western Europe and Scandinavia. Wellcome also have extensive subsidiaries, several of them undertaking secondary manufacture. Japanese companies are moving quickly into the pharmaceutical industry, and while Wellcome, like most companies, have found it difficult to enter into the pharmaceutical industry in Japan itself, they have established a marketing and distribution presence in that country.

Glaxo have tended not to license production in the past, but there is a large amount of bartering in the industry – one company markets a drug for another. Previously Glaxo serviced the American market by granting marketing licences for their own home-produced products because of the enormous cost of establishing a marketing operation there. Now however Glaxo have started to market under their own name in the USA. Although they have no secondary production at the moment, a new secondary production greenfield plant is to be opened in late 1984. Glaxo are also involved in a certain amount of bulk trade in active ingredients (mostly penicillin). Glaxo sell to other companies who formulate the product into their own branded preparations. Wellcome have licensed production occasionally for strategic reasons, but in general they prefer to manufacture on their own account.

Worldwide, the pharmaceutical industry has reached maturity and there is strong competition and sometimes over-capacity. There is very fierce competition in the introduction of new drugs, and both Glaxo and Wellcome have been successful in discovering important new drugs in recent years. These have been the basis of their worldwide manufacturing activities.

BP Chemicals

The chemical industry, as represented by British Petroleum, is substantially different from the pharmaceutical industry, although here also research is very important.

BP's interest in chemicals started in the early 1950s when they formed three joint companies – with Distillers in the UK, with Bayer in West Germany and with Pechiney/Kuhlmann in France. These joint arrangements were undertaken because BP did not have the chemical expertise; this was to be supplied by their partners who also secured rights to offtake finished chemical products manufactured by the joint company. BP's corresponding contribution was to supply the feedstock and fuels and to absorb the oil products derived from the cracking operations. These arrangements variously influenced the location of the plants. In the UK and France they were built on sites next to BP refineries, while in Germany the choice of a site near Cologne was dictated by proximity to Bayer's main operations.

The next significant expansion came in 1967 when BP acquired Distillers' chemical and plastics interests and took over full ownership of the UK joint venture. For BP the move signified a further extension of their business, since Distillers were major manufacturers of PVC and were involved in ethanol-based chemical processes. They originally made acetic acid from an ethanol base but since then other processes have been developed for acetic acid.

In the early 1970s significant investments were made in ethylene and downstream capacity in the UK, France and West Germany. The general strategy was one of diversification into downstream activities in the light of what appeared to be assured market growth. In the later 1970s plans were drawn up for further expansions. Some projects were however delayed and eventually abandoned as the rapid market growth of the early 1970s gave way to more modest growth following the oil price increases. The industry is now characterized by substantial over-capacity.

It was felt in the 1970s that BP were too UK based and too commodity orientated, and needed extra outlets for their ethylene production. In 1978–9 BP acquired two companies – one in Antwerp from Union Carbide and a polystyrene plant at Wingles in France from Monsanto. They also restructured their French associate Naphtachimie, converting the cracking operation to a form of asset-sharing partnership and acquiring full ownership of the ethylene derivative plants and businesses.

BP's long term objectives are to reshape its chemical operations by rationalization and reconstruction, by disposing of plants and business-es which cannot be seen to have a viable long-term future, by maintaining competitive parity of its technical resource to protect its well-established operations, and by reducing progressively its dependence on commodity chemicals and moving into specialist product areas.

The pursuit of this policy has already seen the permanent closure of a score of plants during the past three years, mostly in the UK but also including plants in France and Belgium. It has also seen the implementation of a portfolio exchange of assets with ICI in the UK, the acquisition of Verdugt NV in Holland – a substantial producer of salts of organic acids – and increases in production capacity for speciality products, such as polymer polyoils and hydroxyethyl cellulose at Antwerp.

The BP Chemicals Group is very much an international firm rather than a collection of national companies, because of the structural nature of the chemical industry. Industrial chemicals trade in international markets and economies of scale are such that production facilities are designed on a pan-European basis. There are significant product transfers between sites, and a major proportion of Antwerp ethylene and Wingles styrene requirements are met from UK operations.

The location of BP's chemical interests has been largely determined by historical factors. The original strategy was to exploit the chemical market potential of the naphtha fraction from oil refining, hence the decision to establish the three initial ventures. These ventures have since been brought into ownership and restructured or otherwise extended, and suitable companies have later been acquired to reshape the product/technology portfolio in the direction of increased specialization. The acquisitions from Union Carbide and Monsanto, for example, were of companies which fitted into BP Chemicals' strategic downstream needs. They were not designed simply in order to gain European market spread.

Britain's accession to the EEC had little effect on BP's operations, since they had investments in Europe beforehand. Membership of the

Economic Community has strengthened BP's connections in directions to which it was already committed. If Britain were to leave the EEC, this would entail considerable disruption to BP's chemical operations.

UK operations were adversely affected in the late 1970s by the high domestic rate of inflation and the high level of the exchange rate. It is not, however, easy to switch production in response to such losses of competitiveness, because the degree of flexibility is small in the short run. Improved productivity and lower inflation have since partly recovered the UK competitive position.

Research and development is centrally co-ordinated, although rather widely spread as a result of inheriting laboratories as part of the acquisitions.

BP have granted a number of licences, mainly of new processes. Licensing agreements are entered into, generally, when the market cannot realistically be supplied by wholly-owned BP production. In some markets, for example in Eastern Europe or Russia, local production by BP may not be a possibility because of government restrictions. In other cases, established competition and market size may make extensive entry by BP into the market too risky in relation to the potential reward.

BP's chemical interests were traditionally linked to their oil interests. BP Chemicals seems to be typical of other chemical firms in that it works on an international basis, with a good deal of inter-trading between its different plants. Bulk chemicals is a market in which there are significant transport costs in relation to value, and many competitors. For these chemicals, therefore, it can be desirable to set up production in locations near to the market. This consideration must, however, be balanced against the benefits of scale (when production is concentrated) which can often overcome transport costs and encourage exporting, and cost and location factors in respect of raw material availability. Proximity of supply has also the less quantifiable advantage that it assists in avoiding national bias and caters for any desire, on the part of the customer, for the security of having a local supplier.

With speciality chemicals, on the other hand, the effects of economies of scale are not significant. They tend to have a higher value in relation to their bulk and are not therefore manufactured in such a large number of locations. Exports of specialities are more widespread than in bulk chemicals. In BP's case there is significant overseas production of specialities in Belgium, the reasons for this being largely historical and associated with the acquisition of Union Carbide's European chemicals interests.

It seems that, in petrochemicals particularly, participating firms should be regarded as truly international rather than as firms based in a particular country with investments overseas.

Addendum

In the chemicals industry we also studied one other firm, which has preferred to remain anonymous. Because of this we are unable to give any details of its type, or spread of overseas investments. In general, however, it appears that in its main area of operation (some forms of bulk chemical products) overseas markets have tended to be serviced by overseas production. Apart from the influence of historical accident, the company cited economies of scale in the production of bulk chemicals, in combination with transport costs and the advantage of proximity to markets, as the main factors promoting overseas production. The same company is involved with the production of some speciality chemicals, but in this case no overseas investment has yet been undertaken. Turnover in these chemicals is not large and any overseas sales are based on exports.

Chemicals: summary

Pharmaceuticals
Overseas markets for primary production (active ingredients) mainly serviced by exporting, except where government regulations require local manufacture. Overseas markets for secondary production often serviced by overseas production.

1 *Principal reasons for overseas production* (Secondary manufacture)
Government regulations and trade restrictions. Advantages of proximity to markets.

2 *Method*
Acquisition and greenfield investment.

3 *Location*
Worldwide.

4 *Type of product*
High technology, based on patents. High value-added.

Chemicals
Overseas markets of speciality chemicals usually serviced by exports. Overseas markets for bulk chemicals usually serviced by overseas production, with some exports.

1 *Principal reasons for overseas production*
Transport costs. Advantages of proximity to markets. Acquisition of know-how. Historical accident.

2 *Method*
Acquisition.

3 *Location*
Europe and worldwide.

4 *Type of product*
   Low and medium technology. Low and medium value-added. Large
   volumes.

V Mechanical and instrument engineering (including motor vehicle components)

This is an industry in which many firms carry out similar types of process, but produce substantially different products. Their attitude towards overseas investment depends to a considerable extent on the exact products that they produce and on historical circumstances. We studied four companies in this category – Guest, Keen & Nettlefolds, Tube Investments, Smiths Industries and the AE Group (Associated Engineering). It will be convenient first to consider each of these separately, although only briefly, and then to see whether there are any overall similarities.

Guest, Keen & Nettlefolds (GKN)

At its foundation (1901–2) GKN was an iron and steel maker with forward integration into steel-derived products: rods, bars, wires, fasteners and a great variety of metal parts for the engineering and construction industries. The merger with Lysaght's (1919) extended steel-making interests into flat products, and manufacturing interests into pressings, hollow-wares and fabrications. Expansion of the British motor industry in the 1920s and 1930s, and again in the late 1950s and 1960s, provided the basis for GKN's growth as a supplier of original equipment to vehicle manufacturers including engine and transmission parts (mainly forgings and castings) and chassis parts (mainly pressings and fabrications).

From the late 1950s GKN became first a supplier of universal joints and drive shafts, and then became concerned with the constant-velocity (CV) joints required for efficient small front-wheel drive vehicles. The Austin 'Mini', designed by Sir Alec Issigonis and launched commercially in the UK in 1959, was the first of these cars. Conversion of the European car markets to front-wheel drive had begun by the 1970s, closely followed by Japan, and later by the USA.

By the time GKN's steel-making interests were nationalized (1967), vehicle components constituted GKN's largest business area. The trend of vehicle design towards the front-wheel drive ensured that CV joints and shafts became the most significant product group internationally.

GKN's expertise in both design and manufacture, backed by patents, was significantly strengthened by the acquisition of Birfield Industries in 1967. Birfield had a minority interest in a German company, Uni-Cardan, specializing in drive joints and shafts, and was well placed to benefit from the introduction of front-wheel drive in Europe. As a result, GKN established a clear technological and market lead in this field in the 1970s.

Apart from some early ventures in some Old Commonwealth countries (India and Australia were the most significant) GKN tended to pursue a policy of satisfying overseas demand by exporting from the UK, rather than by overseas investment. Efforts to increase exports in the 1960s and early 1970s met with modest success, but experience both in the UK companies and in Uni-Cardan showed that export potentials for motor components were mostly lower than GKN had been expecting. 'Local content' rules were sometimes being operated but, even where they were not, the main customers (the vehicle builders) almost invariably had marked preferences for buying from local production sources. As mass producers, they placed great weight on such factors as continuity and security of supply, ease of communication about commercial and technical matters, comparable cost structures and cost trends, and familiarity with technical standards – all of which tend to favour domestic suppliers, at least for the bulk of the purchases. Use was made of overseas suppliers to satisfy minor (sometimes non-standard) requirements, and to keep track of component costs and qualities available to other vehicle builders and competitors.

Uni-Cardan had consequently been investing in production facilities outside Germany, to supply the growing national industries in Europe. In GKN's view, the emerging demand for front-wheel drive components required a continuation of this strategy, and they supported growing investments in Germany, France, Italy and Sweden while also purchasing further shareholdings in Uni-Cardan. Both forms of investment were financed by retentions and overseas borrowings. GKN similarly took shareholdings in Spanish and Mexican companies.

North America has been an area of more recent importance for GKN's overseas investments. The interest of American-based vehicle producers in introducing European-style cars to their domestic markets was spurred both by rising imports and the energy crises of 1973–5. By the later 1970s they were moving towards production planning of fuel-efficient front-wheel drive models, and GKN was involved in three different ways.

General Motors had asked for licences to develop and produce CV joints several years earlier: in-house production was, and is, GM policy, as it was, and is, with the Japanese. Both GM and NTN (the leading Japanese producer of drive joints) were granted licences by GKN. Ford also wanted proved drive joints, but the volumes required were such that imports were not acceptable to Ford. However, they were not at the time in a position to invest heavily in manufacture under licence, and so they offered GKN a contract to supply, based on GKN manufacturing investment in the USA; two production plants were subsequently built by GKN. On the other hand, Chrysler, unlike either of their main rivals, were willing to accept imports (at least initially) and they were supplied from the British, French and German factories. Ford quite recently have indicated their intention to move towards in-house production, and Chrysler their preference for local supply.

While favourable developments in automotive fields were taking place in Europe and the USA, GKN's main businesses in the UK (both for motor components and the more traditional steel-derived products) were coming under increasingly severe pressure. The British motor industry was losing domestic market share to imports, and having difficulties both in holding traditional export markets, and in developing new European markets. Other important end-use markets for GKN (for example in mechanical engineering) were also having broadly similar problems, while pressures from direct imports continued to be strong (for example in finished steel and fasteners) despite some sizeable investments by GKN in machinery, methods and marketing.

In these circumstances, GKN has consciously pursued two main lines of policy. First, there has been a programme of rationalization, both at home and abroad, in order to move out of markets which the company regards as untenable. Second, there has been a programme of expansion into selected areas of the industrial service industries. In some ways this began with the company's entry into steel stockholding in 1968, but it has been developed to include (among other things) the distribution of automotive replacement parts and accessories, leasing and servicing of vending machines, merchanting of traditional fastener and hardware items, hiring of pallets and other merchandise handling equipment, and so on. In the specific case of automotive replacement parts and steel stockholding, major acquisitions were the primary routes to market entry. In autoparts, entry into North American markets was given a high strategic priority because of the large market size and the sophisticated nature of supply and management systems.

GKN's strategy remains one of further concentration on a narrower range of higher value-added manufactured products and on selected industrial service. The company feels that future investments will therefore be dictated by the needs and opportunities of these markets, whether they are in the UK or overseas.

TI Group (Tube Investments)

TI had traditionally preferred to manufacture in the United Kingdom and to export. Their direct investment overseas has historically been in the Old Commonwealth, in developing countries (especially in bicycles), and latterly in North America. Europe has never been rated as highly. A depressed UK home market has however made TI look increasingly to export markets. Where possible these markets are served by setting up forward warehouses and sales points. This is so, for example, in the case of Crane, a company based in Slough and controlled (51 per cent) by TI, which specializes in mechanical packing, seals for pumps, etc. In other cases, however, it is recognized that manufacture overseas is necessary. Sometimes this is because overseas markets require specialized products which cater for those markets alone, e.g. bicycles in Holland. Sometimes it is desirable to be near the customer for technical reasons, and sometimes there are nationalistic reasons for countries wishing to buy from manufacturers within their own borders.

In 1975–6 TI acquired a German bicycle firm now called Raleigh Farrahder. This was when Raleigh was optimistic about the possibilities of selling bicycles in Europe. Farrahder has however been left dormant and does not manufacture at present, but bicycle manufacturing is successful in Holland where TI bought a business with a good name at the top end of the quality range. It now has 30 per cent of the Dutch market.

In West Germany, TI had a significant operation in Interdomo – a heating boiler firm – which has now been sold. It was acquired via the acquisition of Midland Aluminium. It is not a company which TI would have tried to acquire themselves if it had not already been part of Midland. It was operated under German management and its activities were largely peculiar to the German market.

TI went into machine tools in the UK in 1966 as a diversification to redeploy funds received for its steel interests. They bought Charles Churchill & Co. which appeared to be a strong company at the time. Churchill wished to expand and it was decided to acquire the German firm Frorliep which specialized in the heavy end of the machine tool range. However, problems developed both with the management of Frorliep and also with the management of Churchill, and Frorliep was sold in 1972–3.

In 1981 TI invested about $100 million in the United States on two major projects. One was a greenfield investment in a high pressure gas cylinder plant and the other the acquisition of a US firm specializing in the manufacture of aircraft engine rings. TI already had a high pressure gas cylinder plant in Chesterfield, which was the sole UK supplier and a considerable exporter to Europe. The US constitutes an attractive market for cylinders, being some eight times the size of the UK market, but it was thought that TI would not be able to sell there unless they were actually manufactured in the country. Hence the decision to invest overseas – to exploit a strong product in search of a larger market.

One of TI's companies was a leading supplier of aircraft engine rings to

SNECMA in France. TI wanted to break into the US market and supply GE and Pratt & Whitney, and they therefore acquired the US firm. Here again it was a story of TI wanting to exploit a situation where they had product strength and where there was a large potential market.

TI partake in licensing agreements in Japan and the United States, but with accession to the EEC there has been a decline in licensing. It is now easier and more satisfactory to manufacture in the UK and to export to EEC countries. In general TI is a strong exporter of a wide range of products to both the developed and the developing worlds.

Smiths Industries (SI)

Smiths Industries divide their business into five operating groups – Aerospace, Distribution, Industrial (including Marine), Engineering, and Medical Systems. Of these Aerospace is currently the largest in terms of turnover, but Medical is the fastest growing. The Australasian and South African businesses are controlled separately, as are some newer small businesses.

The Aerospace Group is mainly concerned with avionics, i.e. in-flight rather than ground-based electronic applications. SI are one of two UK companies who are world leaders in the field of head-up displays. Their involvement in this stems from their acquisition many years ago of a company which had started to develop the technology but were short of funds. SI provided the necessary funds and have built the business up to its present position. SI also manufacture autothrottles and jet engine control systems; the latter through a joint company with the Dowty Group. Lucas provide the main British competition in the market for engine controls.

SI's overseas investments in Aerospace have been in the United States. Initially they set up a product support operation to which they subsequently added production and development capabilities. Then five years ago, they acquired a US company which was manufacturing related products. Exporting from the UK had always been a possibility, but a great advantage of producing in the United States was that SI knew what their costs would be in terms of dollars. They did not have to worry about differential inflation rates and exchange rate movements. Such considerations are important since it is necessary, for instance, for SI to quote prices in US dollars to Boeing for six years ahead. US production is, moreover, very efficient and this more than outweighs the high wage levels that are found there. SI's US companies are not restricted to the US market but seek business worldwide. They export to the UK and provide parts for the Airbus.

The Medical Systems Group manufactures single-use disposable plastic products for use mainly in the fields of anaesthetics and urology.

The largest medical systems subsidiary, Portex, is the world leader in the former, but the field is very competitive. SI became involved in the field when their car heater hose company acquired a two-man operation in Kent over twenty years ago. The Medical Systems Group now includes two companies in the USA – one acquired, one established by SI – two in the UK and two in France. The US companies concentrate on the American market but 75 per cent of the UK production is exported. The biggest single market for exports is Japan. SI envisage the possibility of establishing manufacturing facilities in Japan in due course. Research and development costs are high in this field and SI undertake R & D both in the UK and in the USA.

The Industrial division encompasses a wide variety of interests, including in particular two companies in the Marine electronics business (one based in the US and one in the UK). The UK company, Kelvin Hughes, makes radar and echo sounders for big ships, but has suffered from the decline of the British shipbuilding industry. In the USA on the other hand, SI produce and distribute radar and echo sounders for use in small workboats and pleasure craft, and there business is very healthy. The equipment was originally built in the UK but is now imported from Japan where it can be made more profitably. SI gets Japanese companies to make this equipment.

The Distribution Group encompasses three national wholesale networks in the UK. All have suffered badly from the recession. SI also have distribution companies in Sweden and Denmark. Neither these nor the UK networks are tied to outlets for SI products.

In South Africa, SI have a manufacturing company which supplies the motor industry with heaters, windscreen wipers, horns, etc. In Australia SI have a company which they acquired, and have subsequently expanded, which distributes furniture fittings to manufacturers. SI also have companies manufacturing vehicle instrumentation and heater and air conditioning equipment for the motor industry.

SI's main areas for overseas investment have been the USA, Australasia and South Africa, in that order. They are not involved in Europe to any great extent, apart from their distribution companies in Sweden and Denmark and their medical affiliate in France. In general, SI find that they can either export their products direct to the customer in Europe or else can deal through agents or local distributors.

This lack of investment in Europe is in contrast to many of their competitors who moved into the Continent during the 1960s. SI on the other hand waited until about ten years ago when they made a conscious policy decision to expand into the United States. These investments were undertaken to gain access to growth markets and SI saw them as a natural extension to their UK operations. Australasia was chosen as a second geographical 'target area'. In total, SI made three acquisitions in the

United States – one an aerospace company, one a medical company and one an electronics company which supplies semi-conductor manufacturing plant to Silicon Valley.

At the time of these acquisitions SI's operations in the UK were in a healthy state and they were making good profits even from the motor industry. Latterly, however, the UK automobile business has declined, both because of the recession and because of increased import penetration. SI suffered through the fact that many manufacturers with plants in the UK have been importing vehicles built on the continent and using continental components. The company has now withdrawn from the direct supply of original equipment to the UK automotive industry.

AE Group (formerly Associated Engineering)

The AE Group was formed in 1947 as a holding company for the interests of three long-established firms, Wellworthy, Hepworth & Grandage and Brico Engineering (then named the British Piston Ring Company). These firms were predominant in the cylinder components industry. The newly formed group then began to expand through the acquisition of other companies. In 1955, for example, AE acquired the Coventry Radiator and Presswork Company (since sold). A piston castings manufacturer, Aeroplane & Motor Aluminium Castings Ltd, was then acquired and in 1968 Edmunds Walker, a components distributor. Glacier Metal was acquired in 1964. Apart from the fact that .nis added one of the world's major plain bearings manufacturers to the Group, the acquisition of Glacier brought important footholds in three overseas markets (in the form of longstanding manufacturing licence agreements with companies in France, Spain and Italy).

AE includes a good many operations where manufacture is in the UK and foreign markets are supplied by exporting. AE owns overseas distribution facilities in several territories, which they use in preference to independent agents, since this enables them to see that their own products are given preferential treatment.

AE has manufacturing operations overseas in France, West Germany, Italy and South Africa. In Europe the piston and ring manufacturing operations, now known as AE France and AE Italy, were acquired in 1960 in order to extend the Group's geographical base with a wider spread of customers. In France AE acquired an existing bearing manufacturing concern (the Geneva-based SIC) in 1979. SIC were bought partly to reduce pressures from a competitor but mainly to provide an entry into the French market where they had manufacturing facilities. AE, through Glacier Metal, and SIC produce a similar set of products, and SIC previously had a licence from Glacier for the manufacture of bearings.

In West Germany AE acquired the Deva company in 1975. This is a company which makes a particular type of metal (Deva-metal) which has special anti-friction characteristics in bearings. AE acquired the company in 1975 to gain the technical expertise involved in the production of this metal which is now made under licence in the UK.

The cylinder components sub-group of AE has manufacturing locations in the UK, France, Italy and South Africa. The main products are pistons, piston rings and cylinder liners. Piston rings are not made in France or South Africa.

AE has diversified into a number of other activities partly as a result of a conscious decision in 1975 by a new Managing Director to diversify away from the declining UK motor industry. The Industrial Products Division was set up and the Tempered Group, manufacturers of springs, tools, etc., was the first acquisition. One small subsidiary of this group is in Detroit, USA.

Some 50 per cent of AE's turnover nowadays is engine components. A large proportion of the rest is accounted for by sales of turbine components and factored products in the after-market division. AE's exports from the UK are widely spread in terms of products and destinations but consist mainly of bearing and cylinder products to Europe, Asia and increasingly North America; and turbine components to Europe and North America.

A variety of factors provided the stimulus for AE's expansion into Europe – achieved initially through the acquisition in the early 1960s of the cylinder components companies in France and Italy. First, AE foresaw the eventual decline of the UK motor industry – although not to the extent that has subsequently come about. Second, there was the formation of the EEC. AE had had some prior experience of the difficulty of trying to service European markets from the UK and feared that their sales would be adversely affected by tariff barriers unless they invested in overseas facilities. Third, AE believed that their European competitors were prepared to rationalize capacity and thus realize cost savings which would further erode AE's competitive position, both in Europe and in the UK.

France and Italy were chosen as the target areas because AE's competitors there were still relatively weak. The German components industry in contrast was characterized by strong competitors, and smaller companies suitable for acquisition were not available. Moreover, there was a tacit understanding between UK and West German companies to avoid disturbing each other's markets.

AE have made some inroads into the German market through exports from the UK, France and Italy. They have however been told by a major customer that their present market share is about as large as it will ever be as long as they persist in overseas supply. German manufacturers apparently have a policy that no more than one third of their component supplies should be from outside Germany. In general, motor manufacturers worldwide like to source the majority of their components locally. This is principally to ensure continuity of supply by avoiding long supply lines, dock strikes, etc., but also because it facilitates technical consultation in the event of component malfunction of other problems. This consideration is strengthened by the fact that manufacturers tend to choose indigenous components for use in new designs.

AE still see themselves as primarily a UK operation despite their expansion into Europe. They feel however that they would face a lot more competition if they did not own their French and Italian subsidiaries. Their geographical diversification has, in addition, increased the stability of the Group by reducing the risk attached to dependence on one market only.

AE would like to break into the US market but this is difficult at the present time because the US motor industry is contracting. To capture a significant market share, they will have to acquire existing facilities as and when the price is right, or establish a greenfield operation.

AE grant production licences both to companies which are in markets to which AE cannot gain access, and also as a way of earning money. Many governments, especially of developing countries, forbid the repatriation of dividends, but allow payments to be made for technical assistance in establishing and operating manufacturing facilities. The firms which buy the right to use AE designs and technology are usually, but not exclusively, in developing countries. In developed countries, comparable technologies are more readily available.

Mechanical engineering – general

Each of the four companies discussed have different product mixes and have invested overseas in different ways. It is however generally true of all these companies that their overseas investment really began to take off in the 1960s. This was due for the most part to the realization that markets overseas were growing faster than in the UK and that full access to these markets would be difficult unless manufacture were to take place there. Overseas investment was in general by way of acquisitions, although there were some greenfield plants. The investments have had varying success, but in some cases (notably with GKN) they have been very successful and have actually laid the foundations for worldwide expansion.

It is interesting that some of these companies saw Europe as the natural field for expansion while others turned to the USA. These differences were true even of firms in the motor industry. This was partly because different motor industry components have different potential markets.

GKN's expansion into the USA, for example, was due to the particular demand by Ford for constant velocity joints in that market. In virtually all cases, whether with motor industry products or otherwise, exports from the UK could not have been on the same scale as sales from the manufacturing plants established overseas.

Mechanical engineering: summary

GKN

Overseas markets mainly serviced (a) by overseas production in the market concerned (particularly for automotive components), and (b) by overseas purchasing (in respect of service and distribution operations).

1 *Principal reasons for overseas production*
   Preference of powerful buyers for domestic supply, where requirements are for mass production. Transport costs.

2 *Method*
   Acquisition, greenfield investment, or joint venture, depending on circumstance.

3 *Location*
   Europe and USA.

4 *Type of product*
   Medium technology. Expertise in design/applications and manufacturing technologies. Large volumes.

TI Group
Overseas markets serviced by exports and overseas production.

1 *Principal reasons for overseas production*
   Desire for expansion. Specialized needs of particular countries. Advantages of proximity to markets. Historical accident.

2 *Method*
   Acquisition of greenfield investment.

3 *Location*
   Europe, USA and Commonwealth.

4 *Type of product*
   Varied, but generally medium technology, based on know-how, technical expertise.

Smiths Industries
Overseas markets serviced by exports and overseas production.

1 *Principal reasons for overseas production*
   Generally proximity to markets and relative production costs.

130

2 *Method*
Acquisition and greenfield investment.

3 *Location*
USA, Australasia, South Africa.

4 *Type of product*
Medium and high technology. Based on technical expertise. Occasionally patents. High value-added.

AE Group
Overseas markets serviced by exports and overseas production.

1 *Principal reasons for overseas production*
Decline of UK market. Advantages of proximity to market and resistance of buyers to overseas suppliers.

2 *Method*
Acquisition and greenfield investment.

3 *Location*
Europe, USA and Commonwealth.

4 *Type of product*
Medium technology. Based on know-how. Large volumes/mixed batch sizes.

VI Mechanical engineering (construction)

The company that we studied in this area was the Davy Corporation Limited. Davy is primarily an engineering and construction organization, although it manufactures some machinery. The construction business is divided into two parts, Petroleum and Chemicals, and Minerals and Metals. Although individual companies of the Group seek their own contracts, Davy also pursue a marketing strategy of close integration to try to ensure the best use of available resources throughout the Group.

All of Davy's Limited machinery manufacture takes place in the UK. Within the UK, Davy have a company in Sheffield (Davy Loewy) which manufactures parts of rolling mills. They also have a fabrication shop in Thornaby part of whose output is used by the parent company: they manufacture also for Davy contracts outside the UK.

In engineering construction, the market is seen as being the whole world. In this field Davy Ashmore were, in 1969, a wholly British-based company which undertook work overseas. They took the view, however, that if they did not expand their operations outside the UK, their business would decrease. They decided that they wanted to be an international company operating mainly from the UK, West Germany and the United States. The emphasis was placed on developed countries because Davy felt that subsidiaries in such countries were likely to be relatively safe from arbitrary government action. Davy nevertheless have three subsidiaries in Brazil, two in India and one in Mexico. They find that Brazil is a particularly difficult market in which to operate.

The first major overseas company that Davy acquired was Bamag in West Germany in 1970. Bamag was part of a group that was going into liquidation. In 1971 Davy acquired Zimmer AG from Vickers, Zimmer being involved in the provision of plant for the man-made fibre industry. In 1973–4 Davy acquired an ailing chemical company, Chemibau in Cologne. The German companies were all good technically, but were weak companies and were not well managed. On acquisition Davy carried out extensive surgery. They reduced the overall size of the companies and introduced their own management expertise. They replaced the old management team with new young Germans, trained by Davy. The German operations have since performed well and make good profits. They now operate from Germany all around the world. The German companies possess different technologies which are not available in the UK, and hence they do not substitute for exports from Britain. Each competes in a specific area and provides a specific capability. Davy have gained little general technical benefit from their acquisition of the German companies – only expertise in specific processes. Moreover, they have not learned a great deal about management techniques from their German companies. On the other hand, they have learnt much from their American acquisitions, particularly as regards expertise in field construction projects.

In 1978, Davy acquired the US company McKee. McKee were a company with a lot of technical know-how and the merger brought Davy both additional strength and an introduction into the US market. Half of the funds were provided internally, and the other half were borrowed.

Davy is the biggest construction company in Europe but in the United States there are several firms which are larger than McKee. McKee is concerned with contracts in the United States market, with limited foreign work, whereas the British and German operations are mainly concerned with overseas contracts. Davy are usually called on to construct their plant close to the source of raw materials, and are involved in projects in oil-rich countries: Indonesia, South East Asia, Venezuela, Mexico, etc.

In the past Davy's German company has had a better reputation for delivery than the UK company. However, the UK company has improved since, and there is not now much difference between the efficiency of the German and UK operations.

One advantage of operating from Germany is that the export credit arrangements in that country are favourable. UK export credit arrangements are also good. If a project is financed with help from the ECGD in Britain, then equipment, etc. has to be purchased in the UK. The same is true for German equipment when the German export credit guarantee department provides finance.

Davy and their competitors all buy equipment from similar companies. Competition takes place not only on the price of such equipment but also on the basis of management expertise and on the ability to put together an appropriate financial package.

Davy undertake some research and development in the UK, but none in the United States. All the German companies do some R & D, especially Zimmer who are in a fast developing field where new applications for fibres are plentiful.

Entry into the EEC did not have much impact on Davy since they had already decided to move into Europe. Leaving the EEC would also have little effect because Davy are now well established in Europe.

Davy is an example of a company which has invested overseas very consciously. A large number of countries for possible investment were considered and the choice narrowed down to Germany and the USA. France, for example, was rejected as a source of major investment because the French are chauvinistic and prefer to buy from their own companies. Davy's German subsidiaries are apparently thought of within Germany as German companies and thus do not face this problem. Many of the firms we have studied have indeed said that their subsidiaries tend to be regarded as natives of the countries in which they find themselves, and are therefore not subject to discrimination.

Davy, as a civil engineering firm, invests overseas in a rather special sense. Davy's American subsidiary does in fact play a similar role to that of the overseas subsidiaries of other companies in a large number of industries, i.e. the role of supplying their indigenous market. In the case of Davy's UK and German companies, on the other hand, the national base is used as an administrative headquarters where projects concerning the whole world are organized. The availability of finance is an important consideration in determining the location of these administrative headquarters. In addition, there is the need to have highly skilled technicians and managers. All construction companies rely to a considerable extent on management and labour in the countries in which construction is actually carried out, but planning, research and top management can be found to the required standard in a small number of countries only. It is in these countries therefore where the headquarters of large civil engineering companies are to be found.

VII Textiles, leather, clothing and footwear

In this classification, we consider only one company, Coats Patons, which is involved in the textiles and clothing industries. Coats Patons is a long-established company which has been investing overseas for more than a hundred years. It provides an interesting case study despite the fact that most of its overseas manufacturing facilities were first established some time before the period on which we are focusing.

Coats Patons

The principal activities of the Coats Patons Group, as described in the Annual Report for 1981 are 'the production and sale of cotton and synthetic threads, industrial yarns, fabrics and hand knittings, fashion garments, knitwear and children's wear'.

A large proportion of Coats Patons' turnover in 1980 was provided by finished garments, embroidery, hand knittings and crafts. Yet the company is perhaps best known for its sewing thread, of which it is the world's largest manufacturer. Indeed, the production of thread might well be said to be the traditional business of the original Coats company. In the early nineteenth century, the Coats family (and their neighbours in Paisley, Scotland – the Clark family) developed a six-cord cotton thread as an acceptable but cheaper alternative to the silk and linen threads already in use. The new product proved successful and sales expanded rapidly, not just in the United Kingdom, but also in America and other countries.

The growth in sales brought concomitant competition from other manufacturers, as thread is a relatively simple product to make. Nevertheless, Coats continued to expand and service overseas markets from their factory at Paisley. In the 1860s, however, the US government imposed tariff barriers against the import of thread. In order to protect what had become a sizeable market for their products, Coats were obliged to manufacture locally and so they bought (in 1870) an American firm, the Conant Winding Company. This was Coats' first overseas investment. Conant were a small operation at the time but were built up by Coats after the acquisition. By 1890 – when Coats became a publicly quoted company – mills had also been established in Russia, Austria, and Canada.

In 1896, Coats merged with Clarks and two smaller English companies, Brook and Chadwick. There followed a period of rapid expansion into overseas markets. By the outbreak of the First World War, manufacturing operations had been established in much of Europe – Poland, Romania, Belgium, Italy, Spain, Switzerland, Portugal, Czechoslovakia and Hungary – as well as in other countries such as Mexico, Japan and Brazil. The Russian mill was expropriated in 1919 and the other Eastern European subsidiaries were lost at the end of the Second World War. The period between the wars saw a slackening of the pace of overseas investment but mills were still purchased or established in France, Holland, Bulgaria, China, Argentina and Germany.

All the above countries had previously been export markets for Coats. The decision to establish local manufacturing facilities was influenced by the imposition of tariff barriers by the host governments. Moreover, this pattern was continued after the Second World War when many of the smaller and less-developed countries also began to impose tariffs on imports. Coats consequently established manufacturing operations in much of Latin America, India and most of the Far East, including Australia. In general, these were greenfield operations as there was usually no local producer who could be taken over.

By the end of the 1950s, Coats were still a company who concentrated exclusively on the production of sewing thread, and they had manufacturing operations in most of the countries of the world. Yet there are significant economies of scale in thread production which mean that Coats Patons would prefer, *ceteris paribus*, to manufacture in the United Kingdom and export. As has been said, however, thread is a relatively simple product to manufacture. Competition takes place mainly on a price basis although assured delivery and goods quality are also important. The incidence of tariff barriers means that exporting from the United Kingdom is not a realistic alternative in most overseas markets. The level of tariffs varies from country to country, and over time, but typically they are set high initially while local industry develops, and subsequently lowered.

The gradual movement to overseas manufacturing led to an inevitable decline in the relative importance of the United Kingdom as a production base for Coats. This was thought undesirable but further domestic production of the thread would clearly not have been economic. In 1960 Coats merged with the wool and synthetic yarns manufacturer, Patons & Baldwins Ltd. The merger represented a diversification from the traditional business of the company but the new entity had a much better geographical balance. Subsequently the new company have acquired other firms involved, in a general way, in the UK textile business (e.g. Pasolds, Jaeger, West Riding Worsted and Woollen Mills). Investments overseas have been limited over the last twenty years. One significant exception was the merger, in 1970, with the Australian clothing manufacturer, Bond's Industries. Coats Patons took this step in an attempt to ameliorate the effects of the Australian banking regulations regarding borrowing by foreigners.

In summary, we may say that their overseas investment strategy, and indeed their corporate investment strategy as a whole, has been largely influenced by the incidence of barriers to trade.

Textiles: summary

Coats Patons
Overseas markets mainly serviced by overseas production.
1 *Principal reasons for overseas production*
   Barriers to trade. Advantages of proximity to markets.

2 *Method*
Acquisition and greenfield investment.

3 *Location*
Worldwide.

4 *Type of product*
Low technology, based on know-how. Low value-added.

VIII   Paper, printing and publishing

In this industrial category, we again consider only one company, Reed International. The word 'company' is perhaps a misnomer as Reed is a conglomerate with major interests in thirteen SIC sectors and minor interests in a further six. The principal activities of its subsidiaries are in three main product areas – publishing; building and home improvement products; packaging and paper.

Reed International

During the 1960s, the Reed paper company was a major trade investment of International Publishing Corporation. The acquisition, in 1965, of the Wall Paper Manufacturers and, in 1970, of International Publishing Corporation formed the basis for what is now Reed International.

The component businesses of Reed had been pursuing a policy of geographical expansion since the early 1960s. This expansion had initially taken the form of extensive acquisitions and development of paper and packaging operations in the Old Commonwealth. There were also some limited moves into continental Europe, largely concentrated in publishing, packaging and home improvements products. After 1977 the policy changed direction, however, and there were disposals of much of the paper and packaging interests outside the North European and North American areas, and more concentration on publishing and home improvement development in those areas.

Development in English speaking areas (particularly North America) presented by far the greatest publishing opportunities not only in terms of market size, but also because of similarity of language. By contrast publishing in Europe had many difficulties (e.g. unfamiliarity with local language and culture, slow reaction to changing tastes and interests, political barriers) particularly when Reed might be trying to run a business from outside the country concerned. In Europe, therefore, they took only minority shareholdings in a number of publishing companies, which represented a relatively small investment. One such operation was a joint venture, on a very small scale, with a Dutch company to acquire a Swiss comics publishing business which sold largely in the German market. The project was undertaken with a view to establishing a base for subsequent expansion in the consumer field but it was discontinued, and the business sold, owing to an inability to break into the local sales and distribution networks effectively. This reinforced the view that the expertise which Reed had sought by participating in a joint venture was only available from local sources. In fact, Reed have now withdrawn from most of their publishing ventures in continental Europe, apart from the very successful business in France. Reed are unable to expand significantly in UK publishing as they already have large market shares in many areas and there is little prospect of high market growth – though they have recently acquired a number of regional newspaper businesses to become the second largest publisher in this sector in the UK. All this is in contrast to Reed's continued development of their publishing business in the United States. The growth potential in North America is much greater than elsewhere. They are moving ahead rapidly in a variety of fields such as medical, security and design and the associated sector of trade shows.

Reed's continental European paper and packaging interests are based on a Dutch company, De Hoop, which they acquired in 1973. The subsidiary (which is now called Reed Corrugated Cases Nederland) has since been expanded and, at the end of 1980, had five factories in Holland supplying a variety of products in the fibre-based packaging sector. Exporting corrugated cases from the United Kingdom is clearly uneconomic, because they are bulky and expensive to transport. Generally, each UK factory services a market within a radius of about 100 miles, but competitive action in Northern Europe is largely dictated by low-pricing German manufacturers. In North America, it has a major investment in a newsprint mill in Quebec. Development of this interest is achieved both in producing high-quality products and through the growth of a speciality chemical business based on by-products of the pulping process.

Reed have a building products company – Koninklijke Sphinx – which is also located in Holland and which also was acquired in 1973. Sphinx manufacture ceramic sanitaryware, wall and floor tiles, and refractories. Sales of sanitaryware are largely restricted to the North European market (Holland, Belgium, France and Germany, but not the United Kingdom). Tiles, in contrast, are sold all over the Continent as well as in the United Kingdom and USA. In principle, it would be economically possible to export tiles from a UK domestic production base. Reed, however, do not have any tile manufacturing operations in the United Kingdom and so are content to service the overseas markets from the Dutch factory. They do export other building products (plastic pipes, sanitaryware, shower fittings) which they manufacture in the United Kingdom. In North America, the investment is in paint and DIY products and wallcoverings. Expansion in the US, in paint and DIY, is largely through acquisition.

Paper, printing and publishing: summary

Reed International
Overseas markets mainly serviced by overseas production.

1 *Principal reasons for overseas production*
   Desire to expand/large domestic market share. Transport costs. Advantages of proximity to markets. Culture problems in publishing.

2 *Method*
   Acquisition.

3 *Location*
   Formerly Commonwealth, now Northern Europe and North America.

4 *Type of product*
   Low and medium technology in production, often sophisticated product.

IX   Other manufacturing (including metal manufacture)

This classification encompasses a variety of industries whose main similarity is that they do not belong to any of the other groupings already mentioned! We consider four companies: Foseco Minsep, Metal Box, Pilkington Brothers and the RMC (Ready Mixed Concrete) Group. Despite the diversity of products, all four have the common role of being suppliers of intermediate goods which are sold to other industrial concerns.

Foseco Minsep

The Foseco Minsep Group specializes in materials technology – the development and manufacture of a wide range of additives and processes which facilitate the production and treatment of materials in the foundry, steel, building and construction industries worldwide. At the end of 1980, the Group was made up of four principal trading sectors: Foseco-Metallurgical, Unicorn, Fosroc and Fosmin. The Fosmin sector generates little of the Group turnover (less than 3 per cent). Moreover, all of the Fosmin sector companies are based in the United Kingdom and accordingly we will not consider their activities in the following discussion. Unicorn refers to Unicorn Industries, one of the world's leading manufacturers of diamond products and abrasives, which was acquired by Foseco Minsep at the end of August 1980. As this acquisition came at the end of the period with which we are concerned, we will again omit discussion of its operations. We are thus left with two sections; Foseco-Metallurgical and Fosroc – the former making products for the steel and foundry industries and the latter for virtually every facet of building, civil engineering and construction work.

The Foseco Minsep Group as such was formed in April 1969 but its origins are much earlier. The Foseco metallurgical activities – which might be said to be the traditional business of the Group – date from 1932. Growth was rapid, and by 1949 exports were being sold through local agents in some twenty-five countries around the world. It was felt at the time, however, that sales would always be limited if they were dependent on exports from the United Kingdom. Foseco's products are in everyday use. Customers want guaranteed sources of supply and prompt delivery. Such requirements are difficult to satisfy from production in the United Kingdom. Hence, as the markets for their products developed, Foseco decided to embark on a strategy of local manufacture. The first two overseas plants were established in 1949 in France and Canada. The 1950s and 1960s saw further international expansion. Manufacturing facilities were established in a number of overseas countries, e.g. Germany, Italy, South Africa, USA, Japan, Austria, India, Australia, Switzerland, Spain, and existing companies were expanded. The concomitant acquisition of new but related companies led to the creation of the Fosroc sector when Foseco Minsep was formed in 1969.

Geographical product expansion continued apace throughout the 1970s though emphasis has always been on specializing in materials technology. New manufacturing facilities continued to be established, particularly in South East Asia and South America. In all countries, the overseas subsidiaries generally undertake manufacturing activities similar to those carried out in the United Kingdom. There is little intra-company trade but Foseco Minsep do still export to some countries, such as China and the Eastern Bloc.

The essential characteristics of the Foseco-Metallurgical and Fosroc businesses are very similar and we will consider them together. In both sectors, Foseco Minsep tend not to set up local manufacturing facilities immediately they enter a new market. They usually start by importing through an agent, then rent production facilities and eventually, as sales grow, finance the building of a greenfield factory from retained profits or local currency borrowing.

As a market develops, customers prefer assured sources of supply and will usually choose a local manufacturer – if one exists – rather than rely on imports. Foseco Minsep try and pre-empt a situation arising whereby they are exporting from the United Kingdom and competing with locally based companies. Their objective is to be first into any market and thus greenfield investment is usually required as there will be no suitable local companies for acquisition. Exporting from the United Kingdom is thus a realistic strategy only for relatively new products or for new markets. Tariff barriers may also play a part in industrial production in some countries (e.g. India, Venezuela and Argentina).

Foseco Minsep see their main competitive advantage as their technological expertise, not only in developing new products or processes but also in providing back-up service. Here local manufacturing facilities, and hence proximity to customer, again prove useful. The products themselves are fairly complex but tend to become quickly outdated. Research and development expenditure is high and particular importance is attached to the development of new products. In the metallurgical business, for example, 50 per cent of present-day products were not sold five years ago. The changes involved tend not to be very radical but usually entail cost savings through the use of a new 'recipe' – e.g. the replacement of a petroleum-based resin by one incorporating a starch base. Patents are taken out but are mainly of strategic value given the relatively short economic life-span of the products. The best strategy is to sell as quickly and as widely as possible before a competing product comes on the market.

In the past, Foseco's products have not involved any significant economies of large-scale production. The situation is changing and, in such cases, production facilities are usually established in the biggest potential market. For example, Foseco have recently set up a plant in Germany to produce injectable magnesium granules for iron desulphurization. Surplus production, of which there is a significant amount, is exported to other markets.

Metal Box

Metal Box are principally engaged in two main activities, the production of packaging materials and the manufacture of central heating equipment. Metal Box have long been the major UK suppliers of packaging materials, particularly metal packaging to the food and drink industries. The high UK market shares for most of their products have, however, meant that in recent years there has been little potential for domestic growth. This situation has been exacerbated by the fact that metal, once supreme as a packaging material, has gradually been facing competition from alternative materials and from plastics in particular. In order to expand, therefore, Metal Box were obliged to look increasingly to overseas markets. Exporting, however, is not a viable possibility. The crucial consideration is volume in relation to price. Much packaging is a standard, low technology, low value-added product, and price competition is intense. Metal cans are bulky and heavy, so transport costs are high. Local manufacture is therefore essential. Moreover, customers like to be able to specify different shapes and sizes for their packaging, and proximity helps here. Plastic packaging – an area in which Metal Box is developing an interest – is very light. Yet it is also cheap and often bulky so that once again transport costs cannot be borne.

Metal Box's initial investments overseas were in the Old Commonwealth areas of Africa, the Far East and the West Indies. These have been followed in the last twenty years by investment in the United States and Europe. In general, Metal Box have preferred to acquire existing businesses in order to establish a base. Greenfield investment entails heavy initial expenditure not only to establish production facilities but also to develop a customer base. Their European subsidiaries in Italy and Greece were both acquisitions in the late 1950s. Metal Box had not previously exported to either country. Competition in these European markets comes primarily from local companies. The large American packaging companies (American Can, Continental Can, Nacanco) operate predominantly in Northern Europe and, to an increasing extent, in the United Kingdom. In retaliation for this 'encroachment' into their domestic market, Metal Box have recently acquired the American firm Risdon – a manufacturer of cosmetics packaging – and also constructed a greenfield plant in Los Angeles to supply Pepsi-Cola. Moreover, they have also established close links with the French packaging company, Carnaud SA, in an attempt to build a European force capable of withstanding the American challenge. The arrangement is that Metal Box have taken a 20 per cent interest in, and contributed £4.61 million in cash to, Carnaud Emballage which holds Carnaud's metal packaging interests in France, Belgium, Italy and Spain. In return, Carnaud Emballage have taken a 40 per cent interest in Metal Box Europe BV – a company set up to hold Metal Box's interests in Italy, Greece and Portugal.

Metal Box entered the central heating business in the United Kingdom in the early 1970s when they acquired the company Stelrad, subsequently adding to it the Ideal Standard domestic central heating business in this country and the European mainland. It was an opportunity to diversify and move into a potentially high growth market. Further expansion into Europe followed when Metal Box bought the Aga radiator interests which, together with their earlier organizations, gave them businesses in Sweden, Belgium, France, Germany, Austria and the Netherlands. They have since spent £35 million in an effort to integrate and modernize these disparate operations. All the overseas companies manufacture radiators, and some supply boilers as well. Dependent on exchange rate relativities, high transport costs and indigenous competition mean that, in general, exporting from the United Kingdom is not a profitable strategy. Metal Box have, however, built a new factory at Rochester not only to manufacture radiators for the home market but also to supplement local production in the nearer overseas markets. The general recession in Europe since the end of the 1970s has meant that Metal Box have had to slim down their operations somewhat. The factory in Germany has been closed completely, and the market is now supplied from Rochester and Sweden. Many of the other overseas subsidiaries have been partially closed, but Rochester has been maintained to top up supply with exports. It thus appears that a policy of domestic production of radiators and export is possible, even if not desirable on the grounds of profitability alone.

Pilkington Brothers

The principal activities of the Pilkington Group are the manufacturing, processing and marketing of glass and a variety of glass-related products. It is with the production of glass that we are mainly concerned here.

Pilkington had its origins in the early nineteenth century, and has had some presence in overseas markets since the later part of that century. Large-scale manufacture overseas began, however, in the 1930s and 1940s. These early investments were located principally in the Old Commonwealth (South Africa, Canada, Australia and New Zealand) and Brazil and Argentina – markets to which Pilkington had previously exported from the United Kingdom and sold through local agents. The rationale behind these initial overseas investments was that the markets in question had developed to such an extent that local manufacture had become an economic possibility. Pilkington maintain that once local manufacture became economically possible it was in their interests to establish local manufacturing operations overseas. This was necessary to maintain a continuing trading interest in the overseas area concerned and to compensate for the inevitable loss of export trade from the UK. Failure to do this could have led to competitors establishing manufacturing facilities, and Pilkington exports would then have had to compete with a local producer. They would have needed to absorb transport costs, and suffer the additional disadvantage that customers usually prefer local supply, since it is less susceptible to interruption. Moreover, although there are not usually any formal restrictions on imports of glass, many countries are keen to have indigenous manufacturing facilities.

In 1958 flat glass manufacture was revolutionized when Pilkington invented the float glass process. The product combined the fire-polished surfaces of sheet glass with the optical qualities of plate glass; the process had a much lower labour requirement, and reduced manufacturing waste, and was thus much more efficient. To exploit the innovation, Pilkington readily granted licences to the main overseas producers, with the result that the float glass process became the universal method for manufacturing high-quality flat glass. The decision to license production was taken for a variety of reasons. First, the tremendous capital investment which is involved in flat glass manufacture meant that it was beyond the company's financial resources to exploit fully the technology themselves. Second, Pilkington wanted to see the float glass process used universally so as to establish themselves as technical leaders in the field and forestall any other technical developments by their competitors. Third, they feared intensive price competition from the manufacturers of high-quality plate glass, who would have tried to avoid losing their markets to glass produced by the new process, if Pilkington had refused to license.

The predominance of a small number of major companies is a feature of the glass industry worldwide. All companies manufacture a product of similar quality and it is difficult to make significant improvements. There are, however, significant economies of scale.

Pilkington's predominant position in the UK flat glass market imposed constraints on the company's ability to expand domestically, and in a sense made the company vulnerable. In realization of this, the Group undertook a certain amount of investment overseas in order to ensure that it was well established in its traditional markets in the Old Commonwealth, Nigeria and Latin America (the company is now the major float and safety glass producer in Latin America) and to develop a foothold in the Far East and more recently the USA. In Europe, Pilkington's early ventures followed the formation of EFTA and consisted of the construction of a float plant in Sweden and two smallish glass processing acquisitions in Finland and Sweden (both previously export markets). The company's presence in Europe was, however, much less significant than elsewhere in the world, and, particularly after Britain's accession to the EEC, Pilkington were left with the feeling that they needed a stronger European presence. But Pilkington had to wait for a major opportunity to move into the Continent. Greenfield investment had been ruled out not only on the grounds of expense, but also because Pilkington would have had to break into established markets where they had little or no distribution network and where there was already over-capacity. It was therefore a question of making a suitable acquisition. In 1979, BSN-Gervais Danone decided to withdraw from the European flat glass industry, thus putting one third of the industry's capacity up for sale. Pilkington acquired a 62 per cent stake in BSN's German subsidiary, Flachglas AG. Flachglas sell mainly to the German and Austrian markets, but they do some exporting to other European countries.

At the same time as they acquired Flachglas, Pilkington was offered the loss-making Belgian and Dutch plants of BSN's subsidiary, Glaverbel. Glaverbel was a company who had adopted a policy of exporting from their home base (exports accounted for some 95 per cent of their production) rather than establishing local manufacturing operations in the markets to be serviced. However, Pilkington were prevented from acquiring Glaverbel by the German Cartel Office who felt that Pilkington would have established a monopoly through Flachglas production, and from exports from the United Kingdom and the Belgian and Dutch factories. Instead, Glaverbel were bought up by Asahi Glass of Japan.

These developments in the European flat glass industry have meant that the previously existing situation – in which, traditionally, particular companies tended to service particular parts of the European market – has begun to fall apart. There are now six major companies operating on the Continent and Pilkington are facing strong and increasing import competition in the UK market. Apart from their desire to expand, Pilkington maintain that their decision to acquire Flachglas was influenced by a need to protect their existing UK and Scandinavian interests. They feel that it would have been unwise to let Flachglas fall into the hands of a competitor.

RMC Group

The RMC Group is engaged in the production and supply of materials – particularly concrete – for use in the construction industry. It provides perhaps the simplest illustration of why a firm has chosen to manufacture overseas.

Concrete is a mixture of cement, sand, aggregates and water. Mixing concrete is a very simple process which can be carried out on any building site given the necessary ingredients. RMC do not, in general manufacture the cement themselves but buy it from specialist companies. Hence, from the point of view of the customer – the building firms – the attraction of using ready-mixed concrete lies in its convenience: problems of supply and storage of the concrete ingredients can be avoided. In essence, therefore, RMC are providing a service. The simplicity of concrete manufacture, however, puts a premium on reliability – both of the product itself and of delivery (since an idle workforce waiting for a delivery of concrete can be very expensive). Because concrete is a frequently used and highly important raw material for the construction industry, effective quality control of the product is essential, and the ready-mixed concrete industry has established standards for the product which have come to be recognized throughout the construction industry in many countries. The RMC Group, as the leading supplier of ready-mixed concrete, also provide a technical back-up in that they carry out a great deal of research into the different requirements of the product in satisfying different applications.

The original company was founded in 1930 and became a subsidiary of the Australian concern, Ready Concrete Ltd, in 1952. The first 'overseas investment' in Germany in 1955, was therefore a decision by an

Australian company to expand its business in Europe. In 1962, Ready Concrete divested itself of all interest in its UK subsidiary. The newly independent UK company, however, continued to capitalize on the success of ready-mixed concrete in Germany. New plants were established and other European investments have also been made in France, Austria, Eire, Spain and Belgium. In all these cases (and indeed elsewhere in the world), the motive for overseas direct investment was a desire to service markets which were adjudged to have high growth potential. Transport costs are obviously very high for concrete because of its weight. Moreover, delivery over long distances is impossible because the concrete can only be kept in liquid form for short periods of time. Each concrete plant can thus service only a very small area, typically within a radius of about ten miles. There is never any question that exporting from the United Kingdom is a realistic alternative to local production.

Other manufacturing: summary

Foseco Minsep
Overseas markets mainly serviced by overseas production.

1 *Principal reasons for overseas production*
   Advantage of proximity to markets. Trade barriers. Preference of buyers for local supply.

2 *Method*
   Greenfield investment.

3 *Location*
   Worldwide.

4 *Type of product*
   Mainly high technology, based on research and development, technical expertise and patents.

Metal Box
Overseas markets mainly serviced by overseas production.

1 *Principal reasons for overseas production*
   Desire for expansion/large domestic market share. Transport costs.

2 *Method*
   Acquisition and some greenfield investment.

3 *Location*
   Worldwide.

4 *Type of product*
   Low technology, low value-added, based on know-how.

Pilkington Brothers
Overseas markets mainly serviced by overseas production.

1 *Principal reasons for overseas production*
   Desire for expansion/large domestic market share. Transport costs. Preference of customers for local supply. Strong overseas competition.
2 *Method*
   Acquisition and greenfield investment.
3 *Location*
   Worldwide.
4 *Type of product*
   Medium technology, based on patents and know-how.

RMC Group
Overseas markets serviced by overseas production.

1 *Principal reasons for overseas production*
   Desire for growth. Nature of product (transport costs).
2 *Method*
   Greenfield investment.
3 *Location*
   Mainly Europe.
4 *Type of product*
   Low technology, based on managerial expertise.

CHAPTER EIGHT

Concluding comments on overseas manufacturing investment

I Introduction

Although most of our judgements about the nature and causes of British manufacturing investment overseas should be apparent from the main body of the study, we draw together in this final chapter some of our principal findings. We also present a few tentative comments on the possible consequences of overseas direct investment for the British economy.

The picture of international manufacturing firms which we have developed contains, not surprisingly, a considerable diversity of experience. To a degree, this diversity is to be expected and can be explained by differences in the character of the industries in which the firms we have studied operate. It is not surprising, for example, that the factors influencing the overseas investment behaviour of pharmaceutical companies should be different from those influencing a firm which supplies lighting equipment. In addition, some variation between firms can certainly be explained by genuine differences in managerial preferences or strategy. Some companies have a deliberate strategy of concentrating, for example, on Europe, while others prefer to concentrate on the USA or the Commonwealth. Some companies also have a greater resistance to overseas investment than others, preferring where possible to concentrate on exporting. Apart from these relatively straightforward reasons for differences in strategy between our firms, a significant element in the diversity of experience we have encountered can be explained by the particular historical evolution of individual companies.

History may exert its influence in a general or a particular fashion. In chapter 4, when we considered the historical development of overseas manufacturing investment, we saw that there were several trends in operation which implied a general influence on many firms. The trade restrictions of the inter-war years, for example, led to a general tendency towards overseas manufacture in developed industrial countries by British firms, particularly in the Commonwealth, while a similar influence was in operation over the early post-war years in developing countries. In both of these cases, the influences in operation had an immediate effect, in that they promoted overseas investment at the time, and a subsequent long-lasting effect, in that they laid down an industrial and geographical structure of production which influenced the firm's strategy for many years to come.

While these broad influences are important in explaining trends in overseas manufacturing, we have also seen a number of examples in chapter 7 of the influence of particular historical circumstances in explaining some of the diversity within trends. For example, although the current production strategies of the firms we have studied in the electrical engineering and the pharmaceutical industries have a number of common features, which we consider later, the firms' current strategies also depend upon the peculiarities of their early development, with the result that some of them have a heavy involvement in the USA (for example Racal and Wellcome) while the Commonwealth is more important for others (for example Glaxo).

Although the diversity of experience between firms we have mentioned does exist, we believe nevertheless that some important generalizations about British manufacturing overseas have been suggested by our study.

II The nature of overseas manufacturing

The sample of firms we have studied is, as far as we can judge, reasonably typical of British firms that undertake significant overseas manufacture. Our firms are, by average British standards, large and dynamic firms for whom the desire for growth is a strong motivating factor. Many of the firms had (and have) significant domestic market shares for their main products. Expansion in existing lines of production in overseas markets was the obvious route to further growth. These overseas markets were typically first served by exports from the United Kingdom, and in many markets exports still continue to be important.

Most of the firms have a long tradition of overseas manufacturing, particularly in the Commonwealth and developing countries, where manufacturing facilities were often established as early as the 1930s. For many of the firms a period of particularly rapid expansion occurred from the early 1960s onwards. While expansion continued in Commonwealth countries, many of the firms made a conscious attempt in the 1960s to expand in the fast-growing American and European markets, relying significantly on overseas production. Licensing as a means of servicing overseas markets does not appear to be very significant for the firms we studied, although there are some important exceptions to this general rule (e.g. Pilkingtons).

148

Concluding comments

The investment and production strategies of the firms have been subject to considerable review and alteration, and we have seen in chapter 7 a number of examples where firms have deliberately diversified or moved out of one area of production into another, have entered and withdrawn from particular markets, or have divested themselves of unsuccessful acquisitions. While this fluidity implies that firms are ready to adapt to changing economic circumstances, we have also seen that in part the current pattern of overseas manufacturing reflects production decisions which were taken in early periods of the firms' growth. In many cases, this early growth laid a 'natural' geographical pattern for future production in which overseas manufacture was a key element. Because many of the firms have had subsidiaries overseas for many years, these subsidiaries have grown to be quite large in their own right and possess some of the characteristics of indigenous firms overseas. Although an initial overseas venture may often have been little more than an assembly or marketing operation, using components, etc. from the UK, a large number of overseas manufacturing subsidiaries now undertake activities which are similiar to those carried out in the UK (see chapter 6, Table 6.7). The subsidiaries often have senior foreign management, are given a significant degree of autonomy in production decisions, and play an active role in identifying and initiating new opportunities for expansion (see Tables 6.8 and 6.10).

We would not wish to exaggerate the degree of independence which overseas subsidiaries possess, since central control can be, and in many cases certainly is, exercised by the UK parent. Important functions such as basic research and development are often centralized, and investment plans may require approval from the central board (see Tables 6.9 and 6.10). Nevertheless, the age and size of many subsidiaries implies that it would frequently be misleading to view them merely as isolated and passive production or assembly facilities, from which production may be switched with little regard for the interests of the subsidiary itself, especially in those cases where overseas capital has been involved.

The firms we have studied tend, on the whole, to operate within one broad industrial area: they are clearly electrical engineering firms or mechanical engineering firms, and so on, rather than conglomerates which spread across industries. As we have noted at several points, within each industrial area there is often a significant diversity of products. There are, however, significant differences in the scope of this: for example, there is greater product diversity in our electrical and mechanical engineering firms than in our pharmaceutical or metal manufacturing firms.

Within this diversity of product it is possible to see a general tendency which applies to most of the firms. We saw in chapter 6 (Table 6.5) that while some of the products produced overseas were relatively new or high technology products with a high value-added, the majority of overseas production was classified by the firms as involving well-established, standardized products, which incorporate relatively low value-added and comparatively low technology. This pattern is reflected in the case studies of chapter 7.

In food and drink, where products are typically standardized, with low value-added, exporting is quite limited and overseas markets tend to be served by overseas production. Similarly, the majority of the firms in the 'other manufacturing' section of chapter 7 – textiles, metal manufacture, glass, building materials – tend to produce established, low technology, low value-added products, whose production is generally located overseas. Perhaps more important, in some parts of those sectors which are usually classified as high technology – particularly electrical engineering and chemicals – a similar trend is evident. We saw in chapter 4 that disaggregation of the balance of trade statistics suggests that electrical engineering firms may have increasingly been producing lower technology, lower value-added products overseas, while exporting higher value-added products. Our case studies show that there are some important instances of overseas manufacture at the higher value-added end of the spectrum, but in general firms seem to prefer to export these products from the established UK base, and are able to do so. In the lower value-added areas, on the other hand, overseas production is more often the necessary or preferred method of market servicing.

A similar story seems to be true of the chemical industry. Exporting and overseas production both occur in most areas of the chemical industry, but in general bulk chemicals are more likely to be produced overseas than are speciality, higher value-added chemicals, which are often exported. In pharmaceuticals also the same pattern emerges, with the greater part of research and development intensive primary production concentrated in the UK, with the lower value-added fabrication of pills, creams, etc. undertaken overseas. The mechanical engineering industry, on the other hand, fits this pattern less than the other industries. In mechanical engineering there is a wide variety of production which often tends to be of medium technology and value-added. The location of production in this industry tends to be somewhat varied, depending upon the particular circumstances of the product, and it is difficult to generalize about any tendency for particular groups of products to be located overseas, with the exception perhaps of automotive components which are often produced abroad.

The remaining matter we should briefly mention at this point concerns how the firms are able to compete successfully in overseas markets against indigenous and foreign firms. For companies in pharmaceuticals and electrical engineering, and for companies such as Foseco Minsep and Smiths Industries, products may be based upon intensive research and development expenditure, may be protected by patents, and may embody a technological lead over the products of competing firms. In such cases, at least in the short run, the firms' competitive ability is fairly straightforward and well defined. In the majority of cases, however, particularly since overseas production tends to be concentrated in established, lower technology products, the firms' competitive advantages may be based upon less tangible factors (cf. Table 6.1). The traditional explanations of brand loyalty and advertising are important factors in the food, drink and tobacco industries, but for these industries, and the remaining industries we have studied, it is sometimes difficult to pin down well-defined and precise competitive advantages. For many firms, for whom research and development is not of great importance, the main competitive advantages seem to stem from their size (which gives them the financial strength to weather changing economic circumstances), their ability to co-ordinate an efficient production and marketing operation and, perhaps more important, the know-how they have gained from a long-established presence in the industry. The companies compete on the basis of the quality and design of their products as well as on price, but this quality and design is based upon the expertise and know-how which has been gained through large-scale operations in many markets over many years.

III The causes of overseas manufacturing

It is perhaps slightly artificial to separate out the specific causes of overseas investment decisions from the matters discussed in the previous section, since the underlying cause of overseas manufacturing stems, in the first instance, from the desire of firms to expand the scope of their operations. In order to do this, it may be necessary to expand into overseas markets, at least after a certain point in time. In addition, it is important to remember that a part of overseas investment at any time is induced by previous decisions to manufacture overseas: once the initial decision has been taken, subsequent investment may follow from natural growth in particular overseas markets. Taking these matters as read, however, it is useful to look at the specific causes of initial overseas investment decisions, in order to see which have been of most significance in practice.

If one had to pick a single factor which, over the long run, has been the most important in promoting British manufacturing investment overseas, that factor would be the presence of trade restrictions in other countries. In chapter 4 we identified a number of periods when trade restrictions were important in stimulating overseas investment – particularly the inter-war years, but also the years before the First World War and the early post-Second World War period. Trade restrictions were seen as promoting overseas investment directly, by pushing firms which had previously exported into overseas manufacture, and indirectly, by altering the spread of operations of many firms so that overseas production became a natural method of supplying certain overseas markets which it was desired to service.

The case studies of chapters 6 and 7 suggest that trade restrictions were also the most important cause (from the perspective of the firms we have studied) of overseas manufacturing during the 1960s and 1970s (see for example Table 6.4). In many ways, therefore, although we have couched our discussion in terms of phases of trade restrictions, one could argue that in practice they have been a continual influence on overseas investment for almost a hundred years. During this time the details have varied, but in the last resort the objective of foreign governments has remained much the same – to promote domestic manufacturing at the expense of imports. Over the 1960s and 1970s, trade restrictions have perhaps relied, to a greater extent than previously, especially in developed countries, on informal barriers such as government-induced purchasing restrictions. In addition, although in less developed markets the tendency may have been to promote low technology manufacture, restrictions in the advanced industrial countries have often tended to promote high and medium technology production.

After trade restrictions, the most important cause of overseas manufacturing would seem to stem from the advantages which may accrue to firms from establishing production in close proximity to the market. Products can be readily adapted, where this is necessary, to suit the requirements of (and changes in) local tastes. Local buyers perceive proximity as implying a safer source of supply than distant production, and one which allows technical problems and individual requirements to be easily dealt with. Local subsidiaries are often regarded as indigenous rather than foreign firms, and therefore preferable to foreign firms. For these and other reasons, firms which have their source of production near to the customer may gain a very real competitive advantage over those which do not.

The advantages of producing close to the market apply to many areas of manufacturing. The case studies suggest that it is particularly important for firms in the mechanical engineering and 'other manufacturing' industries, where the products are often intermediate goods which must be adapted to suit the needs of local producers or purchasers or which, from the purchasers' perspective, require an assurance of supply (e.g. automotive components). In these industries, in which competition is based upon technical know-how and design rather than a clear technical lead or patent, there is often strong competition from competing indigenous firms and proximity to markets may carry significant weight with purchasers.

Concluding comments

The final factor of general importance is transport costs. Eight of the firms in our sample (Table 6.4) consider this factor to have been a very important influence on their strategy. It is clear from the case studies that transport costs are important for those firms that operate in industries (such as the food and drink industries) which produce relatively low technology, low value-added products, or which produce goods from the lower technology and value-added end of the electrical and chemical engineering industries. These products are either bulky or heavy, or have narrow profit margins because of strong local competition, and supply from an export base would be strongly hampered (or rendered impossible) by the extra costs imposed by transport over long distance. We should also note that transport costs were of some significance (although not of major importance) for two firms which produce medium technology goods in mechanical engineering and 'other manufacturing', and for a firm which produced relatively high value-added tobacco products.

While the earlier chapters have highlighted a few other scattered motives for overseas manufacture (such as the desire to acquire a particular foreign technology) the other important factor which we should mention, as much for its absence as its presence, is relative production cost differences between the UK and overseas. As far as we could discern, only two firms, in the mechanical and electrical engineering industries, considered production cost differences an important influence on the overseas investment decision. In one of these cases the product was based upon relatively low technology, with narrow profit margins, and the firm felt that lower overseas costs (at the time caused in part by relatively high UK inflation, in combination with a strong sterling exchange rate) made exporting from the UK a strategy which was not sustainable in the long run: the firm's other advantages were not considered great enough to prevent low cost overseas producers from capturing the market.

It is possible that the responses we obtained from firms may have underplayed the significance of production costs. One would expect production costs to be most important where products embody a relatively low technology and value-added. In many instances, firms have referred to transport costs and trade restrictions as the important causes of overseas manufacture for products such as these. Presumably, where transport costs were important, production costs in the UK were not sufficiently low to overcome these. Having said this, many of the firms (see chapter 6) did not feel able to give a clear opinion about whether the UK was more or less attractive as a production location than similar countries in Europe or the USA. In some instances, productivity per man was judged higher in the USA and parts of Europe, but this was often offset by lower wage costs in the UK, so that unit costs were not necessarily lower overseas. In addition, since the scale of production varies between locations over time, it was considered difficult to judge unit cost differences in cases where scale of output significantly affected costs. In view of this, the best that one can say is that in the majority of instances there was no clear tendency, either way, for the UK to be judged better or worse, from the point of view of production costs, than similar countries overseas. Other factors played the predominant part in deciding whether production should take place at home or overseas.

IV   Investment overseas as a substitute for investment in the UK

In so far as overseas production can be attributed to trade restrictions, the advantages of proximity, or the importance of transport costs, overseas investment cannot be regarded as a direct substitute for investment in Britain. Reddaway (1968) assumed that if British firms had not invested overseas, foreign or indigenous firms would have done so, so that alternative investment in the UK was not a possibility. We have made no such assumption, but have looked at each case on its merits. Nevertheless, our conclusions have similarities with those of Reddaway on this point, since we have found that in nearly all cases investment in Britain was not a feasible alternative to investment overseas, given the scale of overseas activities that was desired.

What we found, however, is that some firms who have invested overseas believe that if they had not done this they could have exported some quantity of the products concerned, but on a much smaller scale than their overseas production. It is possible to make a rough guess at the magnitudes that might have been involved, assuming that our firms are typical of all international UK firms.

About 50 per cent of our firms suggested (Table 6.6) that exporting would have been a viable alternative had overseas production facilities not been established. It was suggested, however, that such sales would only have been a fraction of overseas production. Let us assume two cases – that UK exports would have been 10 or 20 per cent of the volume of their overseas production. Houston and Dunning (1976, p. 9) estimate that industrial output overseas by UK firms is about double the value of goods exported from the UK. On this basis (and generalizing to all international firms) additional UK exports, in the absence of overseas investment, might have represented 10 or 20 per cent (overseas production is double exports, but only 50 per cent of the firms could have exported more) above the level of exports that would otherwise have taken place.

The impact on the economy of an increase in the level of exports of this order depends on the level of capacity utilization. In the period of full employment in the 1950s and 1960s there would have been no effect on overall employment, but only a distribution effect. Higher exports would have implied lower consumption, government expenditure or domestic investment. Alternatively, additional imports could have provided the extra resources, and in that case inflationary pressure on output and employment would not have increased.

In a period of substantial unused capacity, such as the 1970s and 1980s, additional employment would be likely to result from additional exports, other things being equal. If we take 1975 as a typical year in the 1970s, the export–sales ratio in manufacturing industry in that year was approximately 22.5 per cent. Employment in manufacturing industry was approximately 7,500,000, of which one-quarter might have been engaged on exports. A level of exports 10 per cent higher than actually took place in 1975 might therefore have led to a 2.5 per cent increase in manufacturing output and employment, and a 20 per cent increase in exports to a 5 per cent increase in manufacturing output and employment, i.e. to an increase of about 200,000 or 400,000 jobs respectively. This is on the assumption that the marginal increase in exports would have been at the average output–employment ratio. Whether extra investment would have been needed to generate this increase in output, employment and exports is another question. In a recession this seems unlikely. On the other hand, if there were a sustained increase in exports of the order of magnitude that we have postulated, no doubt extra investment would have been needed in the UK.

The conclusion we draw, therefore, is that if overseas investment had not taken place, some extra investment in the UK would probably have occurred, but it is doubtful whether the effect would have been substantial. There might however have been a sizeable increase in the level of employment in export industries. It is less certain, however, whether the increase in exports and employment could have been sustained. The longer the period of time that elapses, the more likely is it that the Reddaway assumption will be borne out in practice. If British firms had found conditions overseas such that direct investment was attractive, it seems likely that foreign firms would sooner or later have reached the same conclusion. The employment effect in the UK might therefore have been in part only a temporary one, even in the absence of full employment.

On the other side of the coin, the absence of overseas investment would have adversely affected the invisible balance of payments. It must also be remembered that a high proportion of the profits of the manufacturing firms concerned are derived from overseas investments. Some of the firms might not have survived without these profits, and if so these particular firms would not have been able to export instead of producing overseas. A decision not to invest overseas might possibly have made the firms concerned more dynamic in the British market than they actually have been, but if this had occurred because of government discouragement of overseas investment, the firms might well have lost dynamism. There are too many uncertainties for reliable conclusions to be reached about this, but the basic fact remains that, in the absence of overseas investment, only a fraction of the relevant overseas output would have been produced in the UK. In no sense has overseas investment been a simple substitute for investment in Britain.

V Consequences of overseas manufacturing investment

Our research has touched only briefly on the question of the overall consequences for the British economy of overseas investment. It would therefore be inappropriate for us to attempt any detailed analysis of the subject. However, since we have referred to aspects of the question at various points, it is perhaps appropriate to conclude with a few tentative comments on the subject. At the very least, these comments may be useful in illustrating how difficult it is to give an unambiguous answer to the question of whether overseas investment has been beneficial or deleterious to the domestic economy.

The large amount of net outward direct investment which has taken place over the post-war period (usually between 1 and 2 per cent of GNP per annum – see chapter 2, Figure 2.4) represents a significant *potential* outflow of funds from the domestic economy. In principle, direct investment overseas could have reduced the quantity of loanable funds available for domestic investment and could have been the source of a significant drain upon the balance of payments. The extent to which either of these possibilities has been significant depends upon how direct investment overseas was in practice financed.

Until the abolition of exchange control regulations in 1979, British firms had to obtain exchange control permission to invest overseas and the finance of any investment was closely regulated (see Bank of England 1967, 1977, Cairncross 1973 and Tew 1978 for the details of the regulations). In practice, exchange control was not intended to prevent profitable direct investments from being undertaken overseas, but was designed to limit the extent to which overseas investment was financed from UK funds (thus preventing a drain on official UK reserves) and to encourage the repatriation of profits on overseas operations. We have already seen in chapter 2 that these objectives were realized – whether or not because of exchange controls – in that the greater part of direct investment overseas has traditionally been financed by overseas borrowing and retained earnings. This is confirmed by the experience of the firms we studied, who suggested that, in so far as the regulations affected them, they did so only by influencing the method of financing their investments – encouraging the use of overseas borrowing and retained earnings. It should be noted, however, that less than half of our firms felt that exchange control regulations had significantly influenced the finance decision: in many instances the pattern of finance would have been the same even in the absence of exchange control. An important reason for this, suggested by many of our firms, is that companies attempt to match assets and liabilities in the currency of each country, so as to minimize exposure to exchange rate fluctuations.

Since exchange control regulations ensured both that the bulk of finance for overseas investment was obtained from overseas and that a significant proportion of overseas profits were repatriated (and given that many British firms perhaps prefer to organize their financial activities in this way) it is not surprising that, on average, overseas subsidiaries of British firms should have made a positive contribution to the balance of payments.

Table 8.1 summarizes for two representative years (of those for which figures are available) the effect upon the balance of payments of identified items associated with direct investment overseas. It indicates that the potential negative effect upon the reserves of direct investment overseas (item 1) was in two recent (typical) years more than offset by the positive effect of foreign currency borrowing overseas (item 5) and overseas earnings from direct investment (item 7). We should note, however, that in Table 8.1 the current and capital account items are put together, so that the effects of current and past items are confounded. In particular, much of item 7, which is the most significant positive item in each period, represents the return on investments which were made in previous periods. As a consequence, as the Central Statistical Office note, 'the results cannot be used to show that gross investment undertaken in one particular period has benefited or will benefit the balance of payments' (CSO 1979, p. 57). Nevertheless, one can say that, over the years, direct investment does appear on average to have made a significant contribution to the balance of payments.

We may thus refute the suggestion that – at least prior to 1979 – overseas direct investment led directly to a shortage of funds for domestic investment. A more sophisticated version of this 'shortage of funds' argument is the proposition that 'borrowing to finance investment overseas could increase companies' capital gearing to an extent which could be an impediment to raising finance for investment in the United Kingdom' (Wilson Committee 1980, p. 246). However, we have already suggested that debt to finance overseas direct investment is likely to be raised in the country concerned in an attempt to balance local assets and liabilities. Taking the company as a whole, gearing may be higher on account of overseas investment, but the asset base overseas is likely to rise over time as profits are ploughed back into further investment, thus making it possible, if all goes well, to generate funds to cover the interest charges involved.

Table 8.1 Identified effect on the balance of payments of direct investment overseas, £ million (excluding oil companies)

		1975	1977
	Capital account items		
1	UK direct investment overseas of which:	−1094	−1790
2	financed by unremitted profits	−969	−1360
3	financed by trade credit, etc.	−53	−302
4	therefore investment to be financed (1 − 2 − 3)	−72	−128
5	net foreign currency borrowing for direct investment overseas	+566	+1287
6	therefore identified effect on reserves (4 + 5)	+494	+1159
	Current account items		
7	Interest, profit and dividends from direct investment overseas	+1583	+2287
8	of which unremitted profits	+969	+1360
9	therefore effect on reserves of interest, profits, dividends (7 − 8)	+614	+927
10	net receipts for royalties, services	+154	+174
11	interest payments on foreign currency borrowings for direct investment	−275	−325
12	therefore identified effect on reserves (9 + 10 + 11)	+493	+776
13	combined effect on reserves of current and capital account items (6 + 12)	+987	+1935

Source: Adapted from CSO (1979) p. 62.
Note: A positive sign indicates the identified effect is to increase reserves; a negative sign, to reduce the reserves.

The preceding analysis deals only with the effects upon the balance of payments of those transactions which can be readily identified from official figures, and does not in practice include all transactions (and influences on the reserves) associated directly and indirectly with investment overseas. The first such influence that we consider briefly is the indirect effect upon exports which may come via the exchange rate.

The net positive and, over the post-war years, rising contribution to the reserves from direct investment overseas implies a net contribution to the standard of living in this country since we are able to purchase more imports than would otherwise have been the case. In practice this is likely to imply an effective rise in the exchange rate, beyond the level it would have reached in the absence of overseas investment, which encourages the import of manufactures and discourages their export. We have already noted (in chapter 4) that over the post-war years there has been a steady decline in the trade balance on manufactured goods – imports of manufactures having grown at a higher rate than exports. We would not claim that this is necessarily due, to any great extent, to the increased net inflows associated with direct investment overseas. Nevertheless, one would expect these net inflows to have contributed – via the exchange rate – to the adverse movement in the balance of trade in manufactures.

It is worth noting that in some respects the argument has similarities with that regarding the impact of North Sea oil revenues. It has been argued in that connection that the increased contribution to the balance of payments from North Sea oil should lead (or has led) via the exchange rate to a decline in the importance of the manufacturing sector (see for example Forsyth and Kay 1980, 1981). In itself this need not be worrying so long as full employment is maintained, since it may simply imply a reorganization of domestic production. Apart from the fact that one's judgement about this matter may depend upon the consequences in practice for unemployment (see for example Blackaby 1980), the main worry which has been expressed in the case of North Sea oil concerns the effects when the oil revenues eventually decline. The argument is that the manufacturing sector may have suffered such a relative decline by then that it would be difficult for manufacturing exports to make up for lost oil revenues, even with the decline in the exchange rate which would follow. While this is clearly an important problem in the case of oil, it should be noted that the situation is different with regard to the exchange rate effect of overseas earnings. Since there is no foreseeable expectation that the latter will decline significantly, there should in turn be no need for a reverse structural adjustment of the kind suggested by the oil analysis.

The second influence on the balance of payments we consider is the induced effect on exports which may follow from direct investment overseas. This matter was one of the important considerations of Reddaway's (1968) study. While the period covered in that study is now quite distant (1955–64) it is nevertheless interesting to consider briefly some of Reddaway's results, if only because these figures are still the only ones of their kind available.

For the sample of firms which he studied, Reddaway estimated that the initial effect of an 'average' £100 of direct investment overseas would be to raise exports by about £9 (essentially because of increased exports of machinery, etc. required to set up or expand the operating assets of the overseas subsidiary). Following this initial effect, it was estimated that in subsequent years exports would on average be higher by about £1.5 per annum. Since Reddaway's basic 'alternative case' assumption was that in general overseas markets would have been lost in the absence of overseas production (see our qualification on this in chapter 6) this figure represented, for Reddaway, the total export effect of overseas investment at the micro level. Leaving aside the question of whether this counterfactual assumption is justified, the export effect estimated by Reddaway represents a straight 'factual' assessment of the effect on exports of a given amount of direct investment overseas. On the (no doubt unrealistic) assumption that the export effects estimated by Reddaway still held good over later periods, it is interesting to examine what influence on this conclusion the more recent trends in overseas investment would have had.

Within the average figure for the export effect given by Reddaway, there is considerable variation both between industries and between countries. The figures for variations between industries (Reddaway 1968, p. 124) do not tell us a great deal, since some of the industries which had a very favourable effect upon exports (for example non-electrical engineering) have increased in importance in the period after Reddaway's study, while others which had a less favourable effect on exports (such as electrical engineering and chemicals) have increased in importance also. The figures for the variation between countries, however, are perhaps of greater interest. Generally speaking, it was found (Reddaway 1968, p. 108) that the most favourable induced effect upon exports came from investments in developing countries and that the most unfavourable effects came from investments in industrialized countries in Europe and the USA.

In so far as this sort of variation is still applicable, the implication would be that recent geographical trends in direct investment overseas, which indicate a movement away from developing countries towards Europe and the USA, suggest that the induced effect on exports may have been distinctly less favourable than it was during the 1950s and early 1960s. We have already indicated that these figures are now quite old, so that we should not place too much reliance on them. Having said this, we should also note (see chapter 4) that a substantial part of overseas investment in the developing countries in the 1950s and early 1960s was connected with the encouragement of indigenous manufacturing. It would be expected that a significant part of the input requirements of many of these then new industries (particularly where the industry was of an assembly type) would have been purchased overseas, and hence would have led to a

160

favourable continuing effect on induced exports. On the other hand, since the industrial countries in Europe and the USA are more easily able to produce input requirements locally, a less favourable effect on induced exports to these areas, compared with developing countries, is to be expected (see also Reddaway 1968, p. 217).

In view of this, one can perhaps have confidence in suggesting that recent geographical movements in direct investment imply that the induced effect on exports, following direct investment overseas, may be less favourable than it was in earlier periods. While we do not have any precise information on this from our company sample, we may note (chapter 6, Table 6.7) that the firms in our sample would seem in general to confirm this conclusion. The activities which most of them undertake overseas are usually similar to those carried out in the UK and in only a few cases are finished goods fabricated from components, materials, etc. supplied from the UK. Most firms tend to source their raw materials and component needs from local suppliers.

The final influence we should consider in connection with the balance of payments has already been mentioned. This is the extent to which overseas manufacturing has involved a direct substitution away from domestic manufacturing exports. Discounting the important influence of historical accident, we have seen (chapter 7) that for relatively high technology products, particularly in electrical engineering and pharmaceuticals, the main causes of overseas production appear to be specific trade restrictions or buying policies, which suggests that the possibilities for exporting would have been very limited. While these factors also apply to certain medium and lower technology products (particularly where governments have attempted to promote indigenous manufacturing) for many of these it is transport costs, tariffs and the advantages of proximity to markets which are the most important causes of overseas production. In many of these instances it seems plausible that a policy of exporting could, in principle, have been pursued. However, because tariffs and transport costs would have led to increased costs relative to domestic and nearby producers, and because the advantages gained from proximity to markets would have been lost, the quantity of exports sold would have been very much less than sales from overseas production. We have made some rough estimates of the possible effects earlier in this chapter. On the basis of these we concluded that overseas production may have resulted in a not insignificant reduction in potential manufacturing exports, but that this effect is more likely to have been short term than long term.

While it would be desirable to present firmer conclusions than we have been able to do about the overall effects on the British economy of direct investment overseas, and to extend the analysis to consider effects other than on the balance of payments, we are reluctant to attempt to do this.

Apart from the fact that the consequences of overseas investment on the economy as a whole have not been the major concern of our study, our reluctance stems from the great uncertainty involved in such an exercise, which must necessarily refer, as a point of comparison, to a hypothetical or counter-factual situation in which overseas manufacture is presumed not to have occurred. Even at the micro level, clear conclusions cannot be reached. In addition, as soon as one attempts to allow for all the possible macro effects – the hypothetical behaviour of domestic profits, output and employment, as well as of exports, in the absence of overseas investment – the analysis becomes very speculative. We would not wish to go further than to stress the effects of overseas investment on the balance of payments and consequently on the exchange rate.

One last subject to which we should return is whether overseas direct investment has been a substitute for investment that would otherwise have taken place in the UK. We tried to answer this question earlier in this chapter. Our conclusion was that, on the basis of the firms that we studied, only a fraction of the relevant overseas output would have been produced in the UK, and that consequently overseas investment has in no sense been a simple substitute for investment in Britain.

References

Abel, D. (1945) *A History of British Tariffs 1923–1942*, London, Heath Cranton.

Aliber, R. Z. (1970) 'A theory of direct foreign investment', in Kindleberger, C. P. (ed.), *The International Corporation*, Cambridge, Mass., MIT Press.

Aliber, R. Z. (1971) 'The multinational enterprise in a multiple currency world', in Dunning, J. H. (ed.), *The Multinational Enterprise*, London, George Allen & Unwin.

Bank of England (1967) 'The UK exchange control: a short history', *Bank of England Quarterly Bulletin*, September, London, Bank of England.

Bank of England (1977) *A Guide to United Kingdom Exchange Control*, London, Bank of England.

Bank of England (1981) 'The effect of exchange control abolition on capital flows', *Bank of England Quarterly Bulletin*, vol. 23, 3, London, Bank of England.

Beenstock, M. (1982) 'Finance and international direct investment in the United Kingdom', in Black, J. and Dunning, J. H. (eds), *International Capital Movements*, London, Macmillan.

Benham, F. C. (1941) *Great Britain under Protection*, New York, Macmillan.

Black, J. and Dunning, J. H. (eds) (1982) *International Capital Movements*, London, Macmillan.

Blackaby, F. (1980) 'Exchange-rate policy and economic strategy', *The Three Banks Review*, June.

Buckley, P. J. and Casson, M. (1976) *The Future of the Multinational Enterprise*, London, Macmillan.

Buckley, P. J. and Casson, M. (1981) 'The optimal timing of a foreign direct investment', *Economic Journal*, March.

Cairncross, A. (1973) *Control of Long Term Capital Movements*, Washington, DC, Brookings Institution.

Caves, R. E. (1971) 'International corporations: the industrial economics of foreign investment', *Economica*, 38.

Caves, R. E. (1974) 'Multinational firms, competition and productivity in host country markets', *Economica*, 41.

Caves, R. E. (1982) *Economic Analysis and the Multinational Enterprise*, Cambridge University Press.

CBI (1980) *Investment Abroad and Jobs at Home*, London, Confederation of British Industry.

Chandler, A. D. (1977) *The Visible Hand*, Cambridge, Mass., Harvard University Press.

Chandler, A. D. (1980) 'The growth of the transnational firm in the United States and the United Kingdom: a comparative analysis', *Economic History Review*, August.

Coase, R. (1937) 'The nature of the firm', *Economica*, 4.

CSO (1979) *United Kingdom Balance of Payments*, London, HMSO.

Dreze, J. (1960) 'Quelques réflexions sereines sur l'adaptation de l'industrie belge au Marché Commun', *Comptes Rendues des Travaux de la Société Royale d'Economie Politique de Belgique*, 275.

Dunning, J. H. (1973) 'The determinants of international production', *Oxford Economic Papers*, November.

Dunning, J. H. (1979) 'The U.K.'s international direct investment position in the mid-1970s', *Lloyds Bank Review*, April.

Dunning, J. H. (1980) 'Explaining changing patterns of international production: in support of the eclectic theory', *Oxford Bulletin of Economics and Statistics*, 41.

Dunning, J. H. (1981) *International Production and the Multinational Enterprise*, London, George Allen & Unwin.

Edelstein, M. (1982) *Overseas Investment in the Age of High Imperialism – the United Kingdom, 1850–1914*, London, Methuen.

Ensor, R. C. K. (1936) *England 1870–1914*, Oxford University Press.

Feinstein, C. H. (1972) *Statistical Tables of National Income Expenditure and Output of the U.K. 1855–1965*, Cambridge University Press.

Forsyth, P. J. and Kay, J. A. (1980) 'The economic implications of North Sea oil revenues', *Fiscal Studies*, July, vol. 1.

Forsyth, P. J. and Kay, J. A. (1981) 'Oil revenues and manufacturing output', *Fiscal Studies*, July, vol. 2.

Francis, A. (1983) 'Markets and hierarchies: efficiency or domination?' in Francis, A., Turk, J. and Willman, P. (eds), *Power, Efficiency and Institutions*, London, Heinemann.

Hannah, L. (1976) *The Rise of the Corporate Economy*, London, Methuen.

Henderson, P. D. (1983) 'Trade policies: trends, issues and influences', *Midland Bank Review*, Winter.

HMSO (1981) *Census of Overseas Assets*, Business Monitor MA4, 1978 Supplement, London, HMSO.

HMSO (1982) *United Kingdom Balance of Payments*, London, HMSO.

HMSO (1984) *Census of Overseas Assets*, Business Monitor MA4, 1981 Supplement, London, HMSO.

Hobbes, T. (1651) *Leviathan*, Everyman's Library, London, Dent, 1973.

Hobsbawm, E. J. (1969) *Industry and Empire*, Harmondsworth, Penguin.

Hood, N. and Young, S. (1979) *The Economics of Multinational Enterprise*, Harlow, Longman.

Horst, T. (1973) 'The simple analytics of multi-national firm behaviour', in

References

Connolly, M. and Swoboda, A. K. (eds), *International Trade and Money*, London, George Allen & Unwin.

Houston, T. and Dunning, J. H. (1976) *U.K. Industry Abroad*, London, The Financial Times Ltd.

Hymer, S. (1960) *The International Operations of National Firms: A Study of Direct Investment*, doctoral dissertation, Cambridge, Mass., MIT Press.

Johnson, H. G. (1970) 'The efficiency and welfare implications of the multinational corporation', in Kindleberger, C. P. (ed.) *The International Corporation: A Symposium*, Cambridge, Mass., MIT Press.

Kaldor, N. (1979) 'Comment', in F. Blackaby (ed.), *De-Industrialisation*, London, Heinemann.

Kalecki, M. (1937) 'The principle of increasing risk', *Economica*, November.

Kay, J. and King, M. (1980) *The British Tax System*, Oxford University Press.

Kindersley, R. M. (1939) 'British overseas investments, 1939', *Economic Journal*, December.

Kindleberger, C. P. (1969) *American Business Abroad: Six Lectures on Direct Investment*, New Haven, Conn., Yale University Press.

Knight, F. H. (1921) *Risk, Uncertainty, and Profit*, New York, Houghton Mifflin.

Lewis, W. A. (1949) *Economic Survey 1919–1939*, London, George Allen & Unwin.

Lindler, S. B. (1961) *An Essay on Trade and Transformation*, Chichester, John Wiley.

Little, I. M. D. (1982) *Economic Development: Theory, Policy and International Relations*, New York, Basic Books.

Littlechild, S. C. (1981) 'Misleading calculations of the social costs of monopoly power', *Economic Journal*, June.

Marglin, S. A. (1978) 'What do bosses do? The origins and functions of hierarchy in capitalist production', in Gorz, A. (ed.), *The Division of Labour: The Labour Process and Class-Struggle in Modern Capitalism*, Brighton, Harvester Press.

Marris, R. (1972) 'Why economics needs a theory of the firm', *Economic Journal*, March (supplement).

Matthews, R. C. O., Feinstein, C. H. and Odling-Smee, J. C. (1982) *British Economic Growth 1856–1973*, Oxford, Clarendon Press.

McDougall, D. and Hutt, R. (1954) 'Imperial preference: a quantitative analysis', *Economic Journal*, June.

Morgan, A. D. (1979) 'Foreign manufacturing by U.K. firms', in Blackaby, F. (ed.), *De-Industrialisation*, London, Heinemann.

OECD (1981) *International Investment and Multinational Enterprises*, Paris, OECD.

Panic, M. (1982) 'International direct investment in conditions of structural disequilibrium: U.K. experience since the 1960s', in Black, J. and Dunning, J. H. (eds), *International Capital Movements*, London, Macmillan.

Penrose, E. T. (1956) 'Foreign investment and the growth of the firm', *Economic Journal*, June.

Pollard, S. (1981) *Peaceful Conquest: The Industrialisation of Europe, 1760–1970*, Oxford University Press.

Posner, M. V. (1961) 'Technical Change and International Trade', *Oxford Economic Papers*, 13.

Posner, M. V. and Steer, A. (1979) 'Price competitiveness and performance of manufacturing industry', in Blackaby, F. (ed.), *De-Industrialisation*, London, Heinemann.

Price, R. W. R. (1978) 'Budgetary policy', in Blackaby, F. (ed.), *British Economic Policy 1960–74*, Cambridge University Press.

Reddaway, W. B. (1968) *Effects of U.K. Direct Investment Overseas* (interim and final reports), Cambridge University Press.

Robinson, A. (1934) 'The problem of management and the size of firms', *Economic Journal*, June.

Schlote, W. (1952) *British Overseas Trade*, Oxford, Basil Blackwell.

Schumpeter, J. A. (1943) *Capitalism, Socialism and Democracy*, London, George Allen & Unwin.

Silberston, Z. A. (1981) 'Factors affecting the growth of firms – theory and practice', in Currie, D., Peel, D. and Peters, W. (eds), *Microeconomic Analysis*, London, Croom Helm.

Stopford, J. M. (1974) 'The origins of British-based multinational manufacturing enterprises', *Business History Review*, 48.

Stopford, J. M. (1976) 'Changing perspectives on investment by British manufacturing multinationals', *Journal of International Business Studies*, vol. 7, 2.

Taylor, C. T. and Silberston, Z. A. (1973) *The Economic Impact of the Patent System*, Cambridge University Press.

Tew, J. H. B. (1978) 'Policies aimed at improving the balance of payments', in Blackaby, F. (ed.), *British Economic Policy 1960–74*, Cambridge University Press.

Thirlwall, A. P. (1979) 'The balance of payments constraint as an explanation of international growth rate differences', *Banca Nazionale del Lavoro, Quarterly Review*, March.

Tripp, B. H. (1956) *Renold Chains*, London, George Allen & Unwin.

Vernon, R. (1966) 'International investment and international trade in the product cycle', *Quarterly Journal of Economics*, May.

Vernon, R. (1974) 'The location of economic activity', in Dunning, J. H. (ed.), *Economic Analysis and the Multinational Enterprise*, London, George Allen & Unwin.

166

References

Vernon, R. (1979) 'The product cycle hypothesis in a new international environment', *Oxford Bulletin of Economics and Statistics*, November.

Ward-Jackson, C. H. (1941) *A History of Courtaulds*, London, Curwen Press (private circulation).

Wells, J. D. and Imber, J. C. (1977) 'The home and export performance of United Kingdom industries', *Economic Trends*, August.

Williamson, O. E. (1973) 'Markets and hierarchies: some elementary considerations', *American Economic Review*, May.

Williamson, O. E. (1975) *Markets and Hierarchies: Analysis & Antitrust Implications*, New York, Free Press.

Wilson, C. (1954) *The History of Unilever*, London, Cassell.

Wilson Committee (1980) *Report*, 2 vols., Cmnd 7937, London, HMSO.

Index

Abel, D., 55
advertising/advertising intensity, 2, 45, 83, 84, 102–5, 107, 109, 111, 112, 151
Aliber, R. Z., 46, 47

balance of payments, effect of overseas investment on, 4, 155–62
Bank of England, 8, 156
barriers to entry, 33
Benham, F. C., 55, 57, 59
Blackaby, F., 159
brand loyalty, 83, 84, 102, 107, 151
Buckley, P. J., 34–7, 39, 42

Cairncross, A., 156
case-study approach, limitations of, 3
Caves, R. E., 2, 31, 33, 42
Chandler, A. D., 39, 56
Coase, R., 35, 37, 38
comparative advantage, 31–3, 42, 43
costs of production, *see* production costs

Dreze, J., 32
Dunning, J. H., 2, 33, 36, 37, 40, 42, 64, 65, 72, 84

Edelstein, M., 12, 45, 54
Ensor, R. C. K., 54
European Economic Community, 87, 118, 119, 128, 133, 143
exchange control regulations, 6, 26, 156, 157
exchange rate: devaluation, 48, 49, 51, 59; influence on overseas investment, 46–9, 58, 112; influence on exporting, 48, 49, 59, 112, 159; over-valuation, 47–9, 58

exporting: as a substitute for overseas investment, 49, 77, 90, 91, 154, 155; effect of overseas investment, 90, 91, 154, 155, 159, 160

Feinstein, C. H., 62
firms: origin, 35, 37, 38; growth, 34, 35, 37, 38, 44, 149; historical context of evolution, 34
Forsyth, P. J., 159
Francis, A., 39
free trade, 53

Hannah, L., 39, 56, 57
Henderson, P. D., 50
history, importance of, 50, 51, 147
Hobbes, T., 37–9
Hobsbawm, E. J., 45, 55
Hood, N., 2, 31
Horst, T., 34
Houston, T., 9, 11, 13, 55, 57, 154
Hutt, R., 57
Hymer, S., 33

Imber, J. C., 66
import substitution, 60, 61
intangible assets, 40, 42, 45, 51
intangible knowledge, 32, 42

Johnson, H. G., 33

Kalecki, M., 39, 43
Kay, J., 159
Kindersley, R. M., 13, 58
Kindleberger, C. P., 33
Knight, F. H., 38
know-how, 42, 45, 80, 114, 120, 130, 131, 136, 145, 146, 151, 152

learning by doing, 44, 92
Lewis, W. A., 55
licensing, 34–7, 41–5, 51, 80–2, 85, 88,
    90–2, 98, 104, 106, 109, 112–14,
    116, 117, 119, 125, 142, 143, 148
Linder, S. B., 32
Little, I. M. D., 60
Littlechild, S. C., 39, 44

McDougall, D., 57
managerial expertise, importance of,
    42, 83, 89, 98, 112, 132, 133, 146
Marglin, S. A., 39
markets: size, 34, 46, 84, 98, 119;
    growth, 46, 84, 98, 104, 117, 137
Marshal-Lerner condition, 48
Marris, R., 39
Matthews, R. C. O., 54, 58, 59, 64
monopoly power, 39, 43, 44, 106, 144
monopoly rent, 43, 81
Morgan, A. D., 21

Panic, M., 65, 66
patents, 33, 39, 83, 88, 108, 115, 120,
    122, 145, 146, 151
Penrose, E. T., 34, 35
perfect competition, 33, 38
Pollard, S., 55, 56
portfolio investment, 1, 5, 6, 31, 45
Posner, M. V., 32, 48
product differentiation, importance of,
    33, 83, 84
production costs, 86, 87, 98, 109, 114,
    130, 153, 154
proprietary rights, 36
proximity to markets, 86, 98, 103, 106,
    120, 130, 131, 135, 138, 145, 152,
    154, 161

Reddaway, W. B., 4, 17, 60, 91, 92,
    154, 159–61
research and development, 2, 17, 19,
    33, 41, 45, 51, 66, 72, 73, 94–6, 98,

108, 109, 113, 114, 116, 119, 126,
    140, 145, 149–51
Ricardo, D., 31
Robinson, A., 39

Schlote, W., 55, 57
Schumpeter, J. A., 38, 39
Silberston, Z. A., 45
Steer, A., 48
Stopford, J. M., 55, 57, 60

tariff barriers, 33–5, 42, 49–51, 54–60,
    87, 106, 111, 134, 135, 140, 161
Taylor, C. T., 45
Tew, J. H. B., 156
trade: influence of demand, 31; influ-
    ence of Imperial preference, 56, 57;
    influence of technology, 32; intra-
    industry, 32, 33; restrictions, 49,
    50, 55, 56, 58–60, 68, 79, 81, 86, 98,
    103, 107, 109, 113–15, 135, 147,
    151–4, 161; Hecksher–Ohlin
    theory, 31; Ricardian theory, 31
trade balance, 48, 65–8, 150, 159
transactions costs, 35, 38–40, 42, 45,
    104, 106, 111
transfer pricing, 36
transport costs, 33, 42, 57, 59, 81, 82,
    86, 87, 98, 103, 107, 109, 112, 114,
    119, 120, 130, 138, 140–2, 145, 146,
    153, 154, 161
Tripp, B. H., 58

value-added, 65–6, 87–9, 98, 102, 107,
    109, 113, 114, 120, 121, 123, 131,
    136, 140, 145, 150, 153
Vernon, R., 32, 34

Ward-Jackson, C. H., 58
Wells, J. D., 66
Williamson, O. E., 35, 36, 40
Wilson, C., 58
Wilson Committee, 157

For Product Safety Concerns and Information please contact our EU
representative GPSR@taylorandfrancis.com Taylor & Francis Verlag GmbH,
Kaufingerstraße 24, 80331 München, Germany

Printed and bound by CPI Group (UK) Ltd, Croydon, CR0 4YY

08/05/2025

01864516-0002